Sleep, Nutrition and Mood

Sleep, Nutrition and Mood

A. H. Crisp

Department of Psychiatry,
St. George's Hospital Medical School, London
and

E. Stonehill

Department of Psychiatry,
Central Middlesex Hospital, London

JOHN WILEY & SONS

London · New York · Sydney · Toronto

Library of Congress Cataloging in Publication Data:

Crisp, Arthur Hamilton.
  Sleep, nutrition, and mood.

  1. Mood (Psychology)   2. Sleep.   3. Nutrition.
4. Psychology, Pathological.   I. Stonehill, E.,
joint author.   II. Title.   [DNLM: 1. Affective
disturbances.   2. Nutrition.   3. Sleep.   WM100 C932s]
RC454.4.C74   616.8′9′071   75–16121

ISBN 0 471 18688 0

Photosetting by Thomson Press (India) Limited, New Delhi,
and printed in Great Britain by The Pitman Press Ltd., Bath

To our families

Acknowledgements

There are certain people whose special help we wish to acknowledge.

In the planning stages of Study 2 we discussed aspects of the methodology with several people. Dr. Miller Mair (Middlesex Hospital Medical School) in particular gave us valuable advice at this stage. The ultimate statistical tasks were both daunting and tedious and we have had invaluable and imaginative help from both Mr. B. Kelly (Medical Research Council computer unit) and more recently Mr. J. Koval (Chelsea College).

The clinical study, which was conducted at St. George's Hospital, owes everything to the nameless patients. They have taught us most of what we know and we are deeply indebted to them for their time and patience. The four consultant psychiatrists, Sir Paul Mallinson (now retired), Dr. M. Partridge (now retired), Dr. R. Priest (now Professor of Psychiatry at St. Mary's Hospital Medical School) and Dr. Peter Storey, were unflagging in their cooperation. They tolerated our demands upon them over three years with good humour, and we now thank them very much. In addition we would like to thank Miss R. Forster, Miss E. Stanger and Mrs. R. Schmidt, who assisted with the interviewing of patients. Dr. G. W. Fenton (Institute of Psychiatry) was a colleague of ours at the Department of Psychiatry, Middlesex Hospital Medical School, when the ideas within this study first took root and he subsequently collaborated with us in part of Study 1, and for this we are most indebted to him and grateful.

The Medical Research Council awarded A. H. C. a grant (G966/180/C) for the period 1967/70, and this was rounded off by a grant from the St. George's Hospital Research Fund for the period 1970/71 (QK269). These funds made the work possible and we are most grateful for them.

When the book came to be written two other people played crucial roles. To Mr. Alan Jones we are indebted for the high quality of the diagrams. To Mrs. Heather Humphrey, who patiently and clear-headedly typed and retyped the manuscript, gradually bringing order out of chaos, we are very especially indebted.

Introduction

It has long been known that disturbances of mood are associated with changes in other areas such as activity, sleep and nutrition. Indeed, within the realm of psychiatric illness these latter disturbances are often prominent features of the various syndromes. Physicians of long ago were particularly attentive to the inter-relationship of these disturbances and also their origins within the individual's constitution.

In recent years the authors, who are clinical psychiatrists, have been particularly interested in these relationships at a clinical level, and with the related and basic problem of the quantification of some aspects of them.

Whilst at times there appear to be disorders of sleep, of nutrition or of mood which are qualitatively abnormal, by far the majority of such 'diseases' reflect quantitative deviations from the norm together with such subtle issues as the individual's level of and direction of complaint.

Succeeding chapters in this book are concerned with these factors within the general population, and also with them within the context of major clinical disorders of weight and sleep and major psychiatric disorders. In each of these specific areas there is already a great deal of research data of a highly specialized kind, both clinical and biochemical, which so far has rarely been mobilized in an attempt to understand the nature of the other disorders. This monograph, then, is concerned with an attempt to clarify some of the clinical links between sleep, activity, nutrition and mood, the impetus for this having stemmed in the first instance from certain observations concerning their interaction in subjects afflicted with primary anorexia nervosa.

Contents

CHAPTER 1

Aspects of Nutrition, Sleep and Mood in the General Population

In utero, the 'parasitic' foetus is relatively well buffered against nutritional deficiencies. Following birth, a clear relationship between nutritional needs, activity and mood immediately becomes evident. The hungry baby is restless and cries. Under normally secure conditions adequate food intake restores it to a state of sleep and contentment. The newborn infant's potential for a rapid rest–activity cycle of the order of 60 minutes is rarely encouraged, and most infants quickly settle to a cycle of the order of four hours periodicity. The time that it takes for the infant to settle further into the natural light/darkness cycle with an ability to sleep through the night is highly variable and appears to be dependent upon constitutional and environmental factors, including parental needs.

The infant's nutritional needs are usually the direct and inescapable responsibility of the mother, and may provide the main basis of contact between them. As the child's perception of the sources of his food and general comfort enlarge so as to include not only the breast or bottle but the whole nature of his mother, and as the mother comes increasingly to expect him to exhibit some degree of independence, the foundations of his experience of interpersonal relationships become laid down. Psychoanalytic theory, and especially Kleinian theory, attaches great significance to this phase of development as an important determinant of adult personality and the propensity to experience anxiety or depression in the face of threat or loss.

Meanwhile, the extent to which the mother meets her child's nutritional needs during the first year of life will be governed by many factors such as economic and cultural values, by the specific importance that nutrition has for her as a person, by her attitude to the existence of her baby and its implications for her own future, and by the baby's emerging established pattern of demand. In many families food such as sweets become part of the main reward systems of child rearing. In such ways then, it is plausible that food can come to accrue complex interpersonal meanings for most people.

Excessive food intake is associated with excessive deposition of fat and weight gain, and in the United Kingdom this is now often related to the excessive intake of cereals in the second six months of life (Eid 1970). Fatness at this stage of development is highly significantly related to fatness (Table 1) throughout later life (Crisp and coworkers, 1970). Such lifelong fatness is associated generally with a high growth rate heralded by an early puberty (Table 2) and prompted at least in part by the high level of nutrition.

The Adult

Cyclical activity

Adult people under normal circumstances have a pattern of daytime wakefulness and nocturnal sleep. This cycle is associated not only with the light/darkness cycle (in the Polar regions of the earth sleep remains much more fragmented in adults) but is also related to Circadian rhythms of a biological kind reflected in 24-hour cycles of body temperature, steroid activity, etc. However, under controlled laboratory circumstances in which people live for some months divorced from environmental cues such as light, darkness, ambient temperature and social contact, rest/activity cycles develop which tend to stray from a strict 24-hour periodicity by as much as an hour or two and in ways which characterize the individual person.

In everyday life most people eat and drink frequently. One example of such ingestion is as follows: 7 a.m. morning tea/coffee; 8.15–8.30 a.m. breakfast; 10.30–10.40 a.m. coffee/biscuit; 12.40–1.15 p.m. lunch; 3.30–3.40 p.m. mid-afternoon tea/coffee/biscuit; 6.0 p.m. tea/cocktails; 7.30–8.15 p.m. dinner; 10.45 p.m. night beverage or alternative snack. The above pattern of recurrent eating/drinking has a periodicity which varies between 75 and 150 minutes and is close to the regular 90-minute cycle of adult oral activity identified by Friedman and Fisher (1967) and Friedman (1968), mainly in institutionalized subjects who were not exposed to the wide range of other stimuli and commitments which characterize the normal person.

Such patterns as the above remain highly variable between people and are again governed by such factors as age, sex, social class, attitudes to fatness and other personal needs. Pathological patterns can arise of which one outstanding example is the 'night-eating' syndrome (Stunkard 1955), wherein the individual abstains from eating for much of the day and then binges in the evening and often during the night. Such patterns, often secret and related to such feelings as loneliness and depression, may be associated with obesity and, implicitly, reduced nocturnal sleep.

Weight

The weight of adult people in our population varies greatly between individuals although, as already stated, it tends to be constant for any one adult. Excessive weight is usually due to excessive fatness, and body weight, taking height into account, is usually used as a clinical measure of obesity. In the present day obesity is commonplace. It is related to age, sex and social

Table 1. Data derived (Crisp and coworkers, 1970) from National Survey of Child Development (Douglas and coworkers, 1969) which is a prospective nationwide study of 5,362 babies born during one week of March 1946.

The table displays data on birthweight related to shape at 7, 11 and 15 years. A close direct relationship continues to exist at all levels. For instance, the fatter children as shown in the table are heavier at birth than the average or thin children and this difference is as marked when their body shape is assessed at the age of 15 as it is if the asessment is at 7. At each of these ages there were approximately twice as many fat children among those who weighed 8 lbs. or more at birth as among those who weighed less than 6 lbs. At 11 years disturbances of puberty temporarily made this relationship less marked

Birth weight (in lbs)	7 yr	% Fat at 11 yr	15 yr	7 yr	% Thin at 11 yr	15 yr
< 6	9*	13	9	24	25	19
6 < 7	12	12	13	23	18	19
7 < 8	14	17	16	17	18	17
8 or more	20	18	19	12	12	15

Reproduced by kind permission of *J. Psychosom. Res.*

* i.e. of those who were < 6 lbs birth weight, 9 per cent fat at 7.

Table 2. Data derived (Crisp and coworkers, 1970) from the National Survey of Child Development (Douglas and coworkers, 1969).

The table shows that more of the fat boys and girls than of the average or thin come into puberty early $x^2 = 503.8$ p < 0.0001), and this association is found even when the body shape is assessed at 7 years of age before the boys or girls show any specific physical signs of approaching puberty. It will be seen that 31 per cent of the boys who were fat at 7 were fully mature at 15, as compared with 25 per cent of the average and 17 per cent of the thin. Of the fat 7-year-old girls 23 per cent reached menarche at 11 years 10 months, as compared with 8 per cent of the thin and 13 per cent of the average.

| | Boys | | | Girls | | |
	Fat	Average	Thin	Fat	Average	Thin
Shape at 7 yr	31*	25	17	23[1]	13	8
Shape at 11 yr	32	26	13	25	13	6
Shape at 15 yr	37	25	11	29	13	2

Reproduced by kind permission of *J. Psychosom. Res.*

* i.e. 31 per cent of boys who were fat at 7 were fully mature at 15 as judged by secondary sexual characteristics.
[1] i.e. 23 per cent of girls who were fat at 7 and 29 per cent who were fat at 15 reached menarche at or before attaining the age of 11 yr 10 months, compared with 8 per cent of thin girls aged 7 and 2 per cent of thin girls aged 15.

4

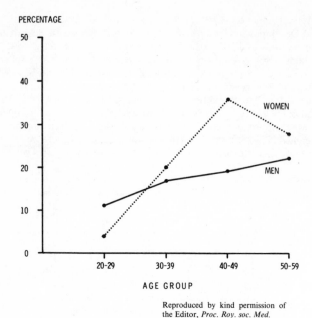

PERCENTAGE

Figure 1. The prevalence of obesity (subjects more
than 30 per cent above ideal weight) in two general
practice populations respectively within the northern and eastern parts of London. The data are
displayed in relation to age and sex (Silverstone,
1968)

class. For instance Silverstone (1968) has shown (Figure 1) that obesity increases
with age in males and also in females up until the fifth decade of life, that
it is twice as common in women as in men, and that it is significantly more
common in the lower social classes (Figure 2). Using a strict definition of
obesity, namely all subjects 30% or more above ideal weight (which is an
actuarial concept defining the most desirable weight as that which is associated
with least morbidity and greatest longevity), he found, for instance, that
over 50% of working class women were obese.

There is a vast literature concerned with the proposition that weight is
related to personality and to aspects of mood. Such claims have usually been
based on studies of highly selected clinic populations and are examined in
more detail in the next chapter. However, from a normal and epidemiological
standpoint there are grounds for postulating a variety of links between food
intake, fatness, personality and mood. In the first instance the interactions
of childhood nutritional and family experiences referred to earlier might be
expected to have woven complex relationships between these factors in the
developing individual. It is evident that whilst some people react by eating
and/or drinking when lonely, anxious or depressed, others react in the opposite
way by loss of appetite and reduced food intake. For some people their relation-

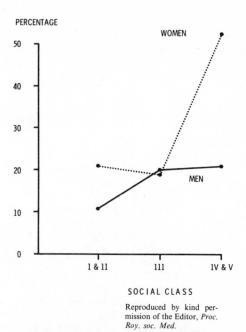

PERCENTAGE

SOCIAL CLASS

Figure 2. The prevalence of obesity (subjects more than 30 per cent above ideal weight) in two general practice populations respectively within the northern and eastern parts of London. The data are displayed in relation to social class and sex (Silverstone, 1968)

ship with food is clearly most important and often appears to transcend their other object relationships including those with other people.

Food, with its burgeoning psychological and interpersonal significance, may well be the principal factor within the nutritional field to have such meanings during early childhood. However, the overall extent of the visible state of nourishment of the growing child, i.e. its degree of fatness, also takes on increasing psychological significance as the years go by, and this becomes progressively and sometimes suddenly the case when the individual reaches adolescence. Weight now comes to mean such additional things as attractiveness, strength and the capacity to reproduce. As already stated, obese subjects reach puberty early, especially females who as a general rule reach puberty 18 months or so earlier than males. Looked at epidemiologically too, fatness is associated with early puberty as well as greater height at this time. By the age of 15 years such individuals, both male and female, stand out from their peers (Tables 3 and 4) by being judged 'more aggressive' by such observers as teachers (Crisp and coworkers, 1970); they are also reasonably enough more likely to reproduce themselves at an earlier age.

It would be surprising if the impact of the age of puberty, i.e. whether it be

Table 3 and 4. Data derived (Crisp and co-workers, 1970 from National Survey of Child Development (Douglas and coworkers, 1969). When the children were 13 and again when they were 15 the teachers assessed a large number of items of behaviour both inside and outside the classrooms. Some of these ratings have been used to group the children according to 'nervousness' and 'aggressiveness'. When these ratings are related to body shape at any of the three ages consistent trends are found. More of the thin than of the fat or average children were described as 'nervous' ($p < 0.001$), whereas more of the fat boys were described as 'aggressive' ($p < 0.01$). This is most marked when fatness and thinness are assessed at the age of 15, that is to say at the time when these ratings of behaviour were made (Table 3). But even when the body shape was assessed 8 years earlier, the thin children were still significantly more likely than the rest to be classed at 15 as 'nervous' and the fat boys as 'aggressive' (Table 4). More of the fatter boys will, of course, have reached puberty at the age of 15

	Fat	Average	Thin
	Nervousness (percentage)		
Shape at 7 yr	12*	14	19
Shape at 11 yr	13	13	22
Shape at 15 yr	11	13	22
	Aggression (percentage)		
Shape at 7 yr	8	6	5
Shape at 11 yr	9	6	3
Shape at 15 yr	9	6	2

* i.e. 12 per cent of children who were fat at 7 were assessed as nervous by the teachers at 13–14 yr of age.

	Boys		Girls	
	Nervous	Aggressive	Nervous	Aggressive
	(%)	(%)	(%)	(%)
Fat at 15	7.9	25.3	14.0	14.5
Thin at 15	17.5	13.6	26.9	15.4
Average at 15				
fat earlier	7.1	18.3	18.3	15.4
thin earlier	16.3	16.8	17.4	12.5
average earlier	10.5	14.2	14.3	16.2

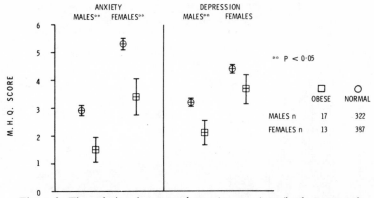

Figure 3. The relation between *depression, anxiety* (both measured on a standardized scale 0–16) and *obesity* (defined from relative weight) in a general practice population in south-west London (Crisp and McGuinness, 1975). Massive obesity is significantly associated with low levels of anxiety in both sexes and with low levels of depression in males. The differences are not accountable for by age.

10 or 15 years or something intermediate, did not itself contribute to the developing adolescent life style and personality. Some years ago Shainess (1961) showed major differences in personality within a group of middle-aged women related to their reported menarchal ages. It becomes evident that if one takes all these factors into account as well as the cultural and social ones, the psychological and social correlates of fatness will not only significantly exist but do so in highly complex and variable ways. Thus one recent general population study (Crisp and McGuinness, 1975) of subjects aged 40–65 years revealed a significant association between the state of massive obesity and lower levels of anxiety and depression in males (Figure 3).

Sleep

Reference has already been made to the way in which the natural sleep/wakefulness cycle of infancy (Gesell and Amatruda 1945) normally yields to the more consolidated pattern of nocturnal sleep and daytime wakefulness in later childhood and adult life (Kleitman 1963). Total amount of time asleep within each 24 hours also diminishes during childhood growth. The newborn infant spends 16 to 17 hours asleep per day, whilst the average adult spends 6 to 9 hours asleep (Figure 4).

There is still wide variation between individual adults and it has been suggested that these are related to factors such as age, sex and personality. For instance, in 1962 McGhie and Russell, in a careful questionnaire study of 2,500 adult subjects of all ages who provided a high response rate and were drawn from various social and educational groups, discovered a number of significant relationships between reported sleep characteristics, age, sex, social class and nervous disposition. The proportion of the total population

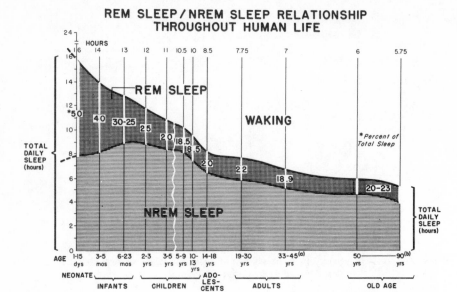

REM SLEEP/NREM SLEEP RELATIONSHIP THROUGHOUT HUMAN LIFE

Figure 4. Graph showing changes (with age) in total amounts of daily sleep, daily REM sleep, and in percentage of REM sleep. Note sharp diminution of REM sleep in the early years. REM sleep falls from 8 hours at birth to less than 1 hour in old age. The amount of NREM sleep throughout life remains more constant, falling from 8 hours to 5 hours. In contrast to the steep decline of REM sleep, the quantity of NREM sleep is undiminished for many years. Although total daily REM sleep falls steadily during life, the percentage rises slightly in adolescence and early adulthood. This rise does not reflect an increase in amount; it is due to the fact that REM sleep does not diminish as quickly as total sleep. Work in progress in several laboratories indicates that the percentage of REM sleep in the 50 to 85-year group may be somewhat higher than represented here. Data for the 33 to 45 and 70 to 85-year groups are taken from Strauch (1963) and Lairy and coworkers (1962) respectively. (Roffwarg Muzio and Dement, 1966)

sleeping less than 5 hours per night rose from 3% within the age range 15–24 years to over 20% in the age range 65–74 years, the increase being striking only after the age of 55 years and being associated with working class people more than others. Taking longer to get off to sleep was also significantly and positively related to age in women such that, in the age range 65–74 years 30% of women reported taking longer than 1½ hours after retiring to bed before getting off to sleep. Again the major increase in this population characteristic occurred after the age of 55 years. Habitual waking before 5.0 a.m. was reported by less than 5% of the population before the age of 64 years but thereafter there was about a threefold increase in individuals who reported so doing (Figure 5).

Reports of 'light sleep' bore an interesting relationship to age. In the case of men 'light sleep' occurred most frequently in the age ranges 35–44 years

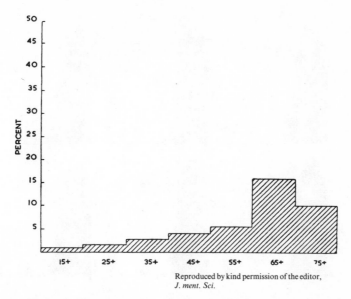

Figure 5. The percentage of normal subjects who report
habitual wakening before 5.0 a.m., related to age (McGhie
and Russell, 1962)

and also over 65 years. The reported prevalence was at its lowest in the intermediate age range of 55–64 years. In the female population there is a more
simple correlation of amount of 'light sleep' and advancing age (Figure 6).

In contrast fewer subjects in the older age ranges reported habitually
experiencing 'morning tiredness'. In McGhie and Russell's study very few
subjects reported sleeping during the day and the authors concluded that
there was a real total reduction of sleep time with increasing age, this despite
an increased consumption of hypnotic drugs in the older age ranges amongst
more females than males. Finally they examined the reported sleep patterns

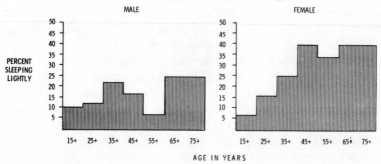

Figure 6. This is the percentage of normal subjects who report
'sleeping lightly' in relation to age and sex (McGhie and Russell,
1962)

10

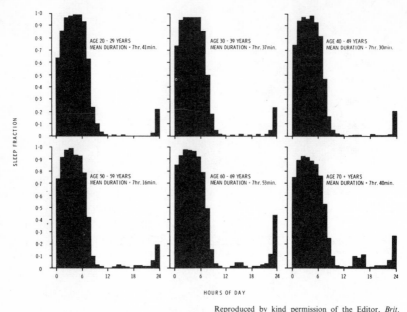

SLEEP FRACTION

HOURS OF DAY

Figure 7. Sleep/wakefulness patterns. The 'sleep fraction' is days on which the subjects slept at a given hour divided by the number of days recorded (Tune, 1968)

in relation to whether or not the subjects reported having a 'nervous disposition' or a previous 'nervous breakdown'. Significant positive associations were found between these characteristics and difficulty in getting off to sleep, light and easily disturbed sleep, and morning tiredness. The authors comment on the main weakness of this study relying as it did for data from self-report postal questionnaires. Nevertheless self-reports by patients are commonly used as the sole source of information about their sleep.

More recently Tune (1968) has reported his careful study of 240 normal volunteers which included 20 men and 20 women in each decade of life from the third to the eighth. One in 20 of these subjects reported sleeping 9 hours or more per day; one in 4 reported sleeping for between 8 and 9 hours per day; the majority reported sleeping between 7 and 8 hours per day, and one in 5 reported sleeping for less than 7 hours each day. He also found that women slept less than men and reported more nocturnal disturbances of sleep especially in the sixth decade of life (50–59 years). The incidence of nocturnal disturbances and midday naps increased overall with age (Figure 7).

In Tune's study the latter gains more than compensated for the former losses in terms of their contribution to the individual's overall duration of sleep as age advanced above 60 years. This finding, whilst according with the EEG observations of Fineberg and Carlson (1968) in older subjects, is contrary to the observations of Lewis (1969) on young and old subjects, as well as those of McGhie and Russell referred to above. Fragmentation of sleep in Tune's study was particularly striking in the over-70s, and he proposed that with advancing age the consolidated sleep/wakefulness pattern is gradually broken down, giving way to the re-emergence of a polycyclic pattern. An increased number of night awakenings in the aged as compared with younger people has also been shown to exist in terms of EEG sleep (Kahn and Fischer, 1969). However these studies have all been cross-sectional ones and it may be that the higher proportion of 'polycyclic' sleepers in older age groups reflects a tendency within these subjects to survive to this age, rather than an intra-individual change with age.

Meanwhile Hartmann, Zwilling and Baekeland (1972) have shown that the personalities and life styles of long and short sleepers are substantially different. Subjects who habitually sleep less than 6 hours tend to be confident, energetic, ambitious and efficient, decisive and content. They keep busy and tend to deny the existence of problems. Subjects who are habitually sleeping for 9 hours or more each day tend to be more isolated and anxious, insecure, sexually inhibited and prone to neurotic illness. Such egosyntonic sleep patterns in the general population have to be distinguished from complaints about poor sleep amongst clinical populations. Most such complaints will be about inability to sleep and will convey the individual's dissatisfaction with his waking life as much as with his sleep. In 1969, Tune found that high scores reflecting introversion on a standardized measure of sociability were related to shorter duration of sleep and early waking in normal subjects, and Orme (1972) emerges with similar findings amongst a clinic population.

Apart from its relationship to psychological traits, sleep patterns are clearly related to immediate factors. Thus it is difficult to get off to sleep if we are frightened or angry, if we are cold, uncomfortable or in pain. The immediate effect of eating a large meal is usually to induce somnolence. Ingestion of alcohol affects people in various ways, but providing it has not induced undue vertigo and nausea its hypnotic effect usually rapidly supervenes, to be followed by a rebound wakefulness.

In recent years it has become possible to examine sleep in EEG terms. Two classes of sleep are now recognized. The first class is nowadays usually called non-REM (NREM) sleep and is divided according to its EEG characteristics into 4 stages ranging from light to deep sleep (the depth being judged by the threshold of awakening to a standard auditory stimulus (Rechtschaffen, Hauri and Zeitlin, 1966; Rechtschaffen and Kales, 1968)). Thus in stage 1 sleep the EEG is akin to the waking EEG. Stage 2 shows a new feature of sleep spindles which give way to slow waves which themselves increasingly dominate the picture as stage 4 is reached. The other class of sleep, first identified by Aserinski and Kleitman in 1955 is called REM sleep and appears to have qualitatively different characteristics from non-REM sleep.

1. It is characterized by low voltage EEG activity akin to that found in stage 1.

2. There is the presence of rapid eye movements (REM).

12

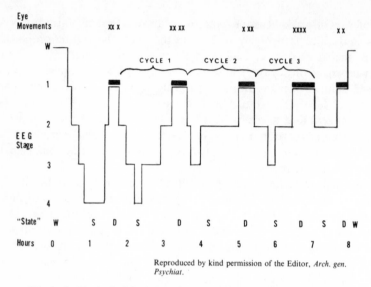

Figure 8. Typical nights' sleep in a young adult (Hartmann, 1968)

3. There is a marked fall in muscle activity as shown in the low amplitude EMG from the chin.

Subjects wakened from REM sleep report distorted mental content indistinguishable from the typical dream, whilst subjects wakened from non-REM sleep often report no mental content or else content of a readily understandable and trivial kind. Non-REM and REM sleep usually alternate cyclically every 80 to 90 minutes in the course of a normal night's rest. REM sleep usually follows slow wave sleep in healthy subjects. Figure 8 shows a typical night's pattern.

Debate continues over the relative 'depth' of REM and non-REM or slow wave sleep. Some argue that REM sleep is a light form of sleep on the grounds of the EEG pattern and the ready rousability of subjects. Others claim that the unrecongnizable mental content (dreaming) of REM sleep suggests that the individual's vigilance system is at its lowest level (Giora and Elan, 1974). Whilst dreaming occurs during REM sleep it is unlikely that REM sleep exists for this purpose or merely reflects it. For instance the amount of REM sleep is greatest in the newborn infant and this is even more the case in prematurely born infants, when information input and experiential factors, the basis of dreams, are at a minimum.

Both classes of sleep are associated with widespread and characteristic metabolic activities. For instance, slow wave sleep is associated with a surge of growth hormone level in the blood, whilst REM sleep is associated with increased peripheral autonomic activity and penile erection in the male. Cerebral blood flow at this time is greater than in the waking state, as is cerebral heat production.

Sleep is necessary, and people who are sleep-deprived eventually become confused and disorganized. They develop an increasing need to sleep and will work off the majority of their sleep 'debt' at the earliest opportunity. Such sleep debts are to some extent selective, e.g. if REM deprivation is relatively induced then the subject's sleep will contain an excess of REM sleep (although up to 40% of such sleep appears to remain 'lost').

Kleitman (1972) in particular has attempted to construe the adult 90-minute REM cycle during sleep as part of a persisting 24-hour 90-minute cycle—the residue of the slightly shorter infantile cycle with its phasic hunger contractions (Wada, 1922) and feeding activity (Marquis, 1941). There is indeed some evidence that this still exists in outline in the awake adult especially in terms of oral activity and cognition (Wolff, 1966; Hartmann, 1968; Friedman, 1968).

Against this burgeoning background of information concerning sleep, theories concerning its purpose continue to proliferate. One substantial view, outlined by Oswald (1970) is that sleep permits necessary restorative and synthetic processes to occur. It would appear reasonable to postulate that stage 3 and stage 4 sleep, with its accompanying reduced metabolic expenditure and surge of growth hormone in the blood especially in young people, is associated with growth and restoration of tissues. Oswald in particular has gone on to suggest that REM sleep is associated with synthetic processes of brain reorganization and repair, of which the concurrent high levels of cognitive (dream) and metabolic cerebral activity are reflections.

Musculo skeletal activity

There are diurnal (Aschoff, 1965) and probably also polycyclical (Friedman and Fisher, 1967) fluctuations of musculo skeletal activity, the latter having been identified with specific reference to 'oral' activity.

Overweight is usually associated with inactivity, underweight with high levels of activity (see next chapter).

Involuntary muscular skeletal activity (e.g. Parkinsonian tremor and the restless leg syndrome) which are still present in stages 1 and 2 of sleep do not occur in stages 3 and 4 (Lugaresi, 1972).

Mood

Little is known about the mood characteristics of normal subjects. Fluctuations in mood, with the experience of such feelings as fear, anger, elation and sadness, are part of normal life. Such affects are regarded as pathological if they have neurotic origins or if they appear to be excessive in relation to the provoking circumstances. Psychiatry concerns itself with such profound disorders of mood which are often labelled anxiety state, phobic avoidance state, depressive illness, etc. (see Chapter 4). In 1971 Crisp and Priest described patterns of *anxiety* and *depression* as two of six psychoneurotic profiles which they set out to measure in the general population aged 40–65. These profiles were based on clinical concepts which had been incorporated into a brief,

14

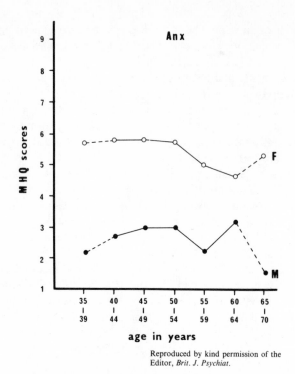

Reproduced by kind permission of the
Editor, *Brit. J. Psychiat.*

Figure 9. The pattern of anxiety in a middle-aged
surburban population (Crisp and Priest, 1971)

standardized, self-rating questionnaire (Crown and Crisp, 1966) and which
provides scores (0–16) on each scale.

Figure 9 and 10 show how levels of *anxiety* and *depression* in this population
are related to age and sex. If anything, levels of *anxiety* fall with age, being
all the time higher in women than in men. Levels of *depression* rise slightly
with age, peaking in the first half of the sixth decade of life in women. Increased
prevalence of obesity, change in weight and sleep disturbances in women at
this time in life, and also the significant association, both in males and females,
between massive obesity and low levels of anxiety and depression have already
been referred to earlier in this chapter.

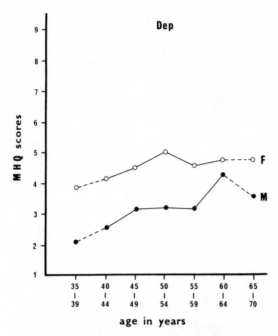

Figure 10. The pattern of depression in a
middle-aged suburban population (Crisp and
Priest, 1971)

References

Aschoff, J. (1965). Circadian rhythms in man. *Science*, **148**, 1427–1432.

Aserinsky, E. and Kleitman, N. (1955). Two types of ocular motility occurring in sleep.
J. Appl. Physiol., **8**, 1–10.

Crisp, A. H. (1967). The possible significance of some behavioural correlates of weight
and carbohydrate intake. *J. Psychosom. Res.*, **11**, 117–131.

Crisp, A. H., Douglas, J. W. B., Ross, J. M. and Stonehill, E. (1970). Some developmental
aspects of disorders of weight. *J. Psychosom. Res.*, **14**, 313–320.

Crisp, A. H. and Priest, R. G. (1971). Psychoneurotic profiles in middle age. *Brit. J.
Psychiat.*, **119**, 385–392.

Crisp, A. H. and McGuinness, B. (1975). Jolly fat. *Br. med. J.*, **4** (In Press).

Crown, S. and Crisp, A. H. (1966). A short clinical diagnostic self-rating scale for psychoneurotic patients. The Middlesex Hospital Questionnaire. *Brit. J. Psychiat.*, **112**, 917–923

Douglas, J. W. B., Ross, J. M., and Simpson, H. P. (1969). *All Our future: A longitudinal
study of Secondary Education*, Peter Davies, London.

Eid, E. E. (1970). Follow-up study of physical growth of children who had excessive
weight gain in first six months of life. *Brit. med. J.*, **2**, No. 5701, 74–76.

Fineberg, I. and Carlson, V. R. (1968). Sleep variables as a function of age in man. *Arch.
gen Psychiat.*, **18**, 239–250.

Friedman, S. (1968). Oral activity cycles in mild chronic schizophrenia. *Amer. J. Psychiat.*,
125, 743.

Friedman, S. and Fisher, C. (1967). On the presence of a rhythmic diurnal, oral instinctual drive cycle in man. *J. Amer. Psychoanal. Ass.*, **15**, 317–343.

Gesell, A. L. and Amatruda, C. S. (1945). *The embriology of behaviour*, Harper, New York.

Giora, Z. and Elan, Z. (1974). What is a dream? *Brit. J. med. Psychol.*, **47**, 283–289.

Hartmann, E. (1968). The 90-minute sleep-dream cycle. *Arch. gen. Psychiat.*, **18**, 280–286.

Hartmann, E., Zwilling, G. R. and Baekeland, F. (1972). Personality traits and life style data for long and short sleepers. *Arch. gen. Psychiat.*, **26**, 463–468.

Kahn, E. and Fischer, C. (1969). The sleep characteristics of the normal aged male. *J. nerv. ment. Dis.*, **148**, 477–494.

Kleitman, N. (1963). *Sleep and Wakefulness*, 2nd Ed. University of Chicago Press, Chicago.

Kleitman, N. (1972). Implications of the rest–activity cycle. In E. Hartmann (Ed.), *Sleeping and Dreaming. Internat. Psychiat. Clin.*, **7**, 13–14. Little, Brown and Co., Boston.

Lairy, G. C., Cor-Mordret, M., Faure, R., and Ridjanovic, S. (1962). *Rev. Neurol.*, **107**, 188.

Lewis, S. A. (1969). Sleep patterns during afternoon naps in the young and elderly. *Brit. J. Psychol.*, **115**, 107–108.

Lugaresi, E. (1972). Normal sleep in animals and man. *Proc. Roy. soc. Med.*, **65**, 173–179.

Marquis, D. F. (1941). Learning in the neonate: The modification of behaviour under three feeding schedules. *J. Exp. Psychol.*, **29**, 263.

McGhie, A. and Russell, S. M. (1962). Subjective sleep disturbances in the normal population. *J. ment. Sci.*, **108**, 642–654.

Orme, J. E. (1972). Duration of sleep and its relationship to age, personality and psychiatric illness. *Brit. J. soc. clin. Psychol.*, **11**, 70–72.

Oswald, I. (1970). Sleep, the great restorer. *New Scientist*, **23**, 170–172.

Rechtschaffen, A., Hauri, P. and Zeitlin, M. (1966). Auditory awakening thresholds in REM–NREM sleep stages. *Percep. motor Skills*, **22**, 927–942.

Rechtschaffen, A. and Kales, A. (Eds.) (1968). A manual of standardized terminology, techniques and scoring system for sleep stages of human subjects. Bethesda; National Institute of Health.

Roffwarg, H. P., Muzio, J. N. and Dement, W. C. (1966). Ontogenetic development of the human sleep-dream cycle. *Science*, **152**, 604–619.

Shainess, N. (1961). A re-evaluation of some aspects of femininity through a study of menstruation. *Comprehens. Psychiat.*, **2**, 20–26.

Silverstone, J. T. (1968). Psychosocial aspects of obesity. *Proc. Roy. soc. Med.*, **61**, 371–375.

Strauch, I. H. (1963). Paper presented to the Association for Psychophysiological Study of Sleep, New York, March 1963.

Stunkard, A. J., Grace, W. J. and Wolff, H. G. (1955). The night-eating syndrome: a pattern of food intake among certain obese patients. *Ann. J. Med.*, **19**, 78–86.

Tune, G. S. (1968) Sleep and wakefulness in normal human adults. *Brit med. J.*, **2**, 269–271.

Tune, G. S. (1969). Sleep and wakefulness in 509 normal human adults. *Brit. J. med. Psychol.*, **42**, 75–80.

Wada, T. (1922). Experimental study of hunger in its relation to activity. *Arch. Psychol.*, **8**, 1.

Wolf, P. (1966). The causes controls and organization of behaviour in the newborn. *Psychol. Issues*, **5**, Monograph 17.

CHAPTER 2

Disturbances of activity, sleep and mood in primary disorders of weight

The disorders of weight to be considered here are obesity and anorexia nervosa. As previously indicated in Chapter 1 obesity is commonplace and requires arbitrary definition reflecting significant quantitative deviations from the mean weight and fat characteristics of the general population. Anorexia nervosa is a more discrete pathological entity but nevertheless has constitutional links with obesity and with ranges of normal behaviour in certain other of its aspects.

Obesity

Obesity describes a state of excessive fatness. Such fatness is easily recognized but is difficult to measure and, in practice, high body weight is often taken as the indicator of obesity. Thus, although it is very occasionally possible to be fat and yet have a body weight of average, normal or unremarkable amount, obesity at the epidemiological level is usually defined in terms of weight greater than say 30% above ideal weight.

However, in medical terms, the degree of recognized and palpable fatness is often considered more important even if the judgement remains mainly a clinical and impressionistic one. Individuals presenting to doctors and being treated for their obesity are inevitably a highly selected subgroup of the obese population. They will include those specifically seeking help for their fatness and others who have sought help for physical or psychological reasons and whose disorders have been attributed to or linked with their obesity by the doctor. It is uncertain how widely the research findings that emerge in relation to this population are applicable to all the obese. For instance information is sparse concerning basic relationships between such factors as sleep, activity, mood and obesity in the general population. Studies have been mainly conducted with clinic populations or selected groups of obese individuals such as those attending outdoor summer camps.

Sleep

The most extreme example of sleep disturbance in obesity may be that found in some instances of the so-called Pickwickian syndrome, a disorder of respiratory insufficiency and somnolence usually associated with massive fatness in which case the symptoms are often dramatically relieved if major fat or fluid loss can be achieved (see Chapter 3). Whilst the precise nature of the primary role of the obesity in this syndrome is obscure it is nevertheless a common observation that many obese people 'snooze' or 'cat-nap' and perhaps also sleep more often than others after a meal.

The Kleine–Levin syndrome is another profound disorder of weight, regarded by some as having a specific hypothalamic basis different from the pathological range of functional hypothalamic disturbances that are also presumably operative in the more common kinds of adult obesity. This disorder is also discussed further in the next chapter but is one more example of the overlap between the so-called clinical disorders of weight and food intake on the one hand and sleep, activity and mood disturbances on the other.

However the position is still more complex. A minority of obese subjects do not sleep excessively and may even complain of insomnia. Of course many obese people paradoxically are in a posture of starvation, having eaten sparingly for many years, thereby avoiding further weight gain despite relative inactivity. Feeding patterns, degrees and kinds of specific malnutrition are legion in the obese. It would be surprising if these were not also associated with and contributory to sleep patterns in a way which sometimes transcended the more global association of fatness, satiation and somnolence.

Meanwhile the data from Chapter 1 reveal an overall increase in obesity in the general population at least until the fifth decade of life in men, after which it tends to fall (maybe through the elimination by early death of chronically obese subjects thereafter), and the sixth decade of life in females. Sleep patterns in the general population have been shown to change in the direction of individuals experiencing less nocturnal and more fragmented sleep as they age. The possibility that such sleep changes may have some links with the changing pattern of growth and weight with age and their underlying nutritional determinants and implications in humans has not been investigated.

Activity

There is an overriding impression that, along with increased somnolence, many obese subjects are singularly inactive throughout the day. Physical muscular activity is an important determinant of calorie expenditure over and above basal caloric needs and, together with caloric intake which reflects the ingestive and absorptive characteristics of the person, plays an important part in affecting the amount of calories stored as fat. This simple statement reflects a complicated situation which has been discussed by Miller and Mumford (1966) and Parizkova (1968) in terms of such factors as internal regulatory mechanisms, environmental cues, patterns of eating. For instance the impact of physical exercise on calorie expenditure appears to transcend the period of exercise and is also affected by the nature of the temporal relationship between it and the ingestion of food.

Constitutionally inactive animals become obese in the experimental situation (Mayer, 1953, 1964) and late onset obesity in the human, especially the male, has been attributed to the drastic reduction of physical activity which often occurs during the third/fourth decade of life and which appears often not to be associated with a reduction of food intake. Inactivity is a feature of some kinds of depressive illness and within this context has been advanced (Stunkard, 1958) as a cause of weight gain leading to obesity under such circumstances.

There are studies which show that inactivity is a feature of childhood obesity and Brüch (1964) has been to the fore in claiming that there is neurotic 'value' in such passive compliant inactivity within the child in the families concerned. Bloom and Eidex (1967) compared the activity of seven obese subjects and six lean subjects. The obese group spent a mean of 15% less time per day standing than the lean group and a mean of 65 minutes more in bed. In other studies obese adolescent girls at summer camps have been found to be less active than their non-obese peers. Such inactivity in adolescence may of course be partly reactive in the sense that the individual feels awkward, clumsy and gross and learns to avoid the ridicule to which she is sometimes exposed if she attempts to join in a sporting or active life with others. Deeper feelings of guilt associated with the feeling that fatness is linked by many with such behaviour as gluttony and shaming aspects of sexuality also arise and lead even more to the adolescent obese person withdrawing from active social life. Nevertheless there also appear to be basic biological influences that excessive food intake and also obesity have on physical activity. Inactivity as well as a frank somnolence follow food intake under normal conditions in contrast to increased activity, alertness and 'pursuit' of food preceding such a meal. Furthermore excessive fatness implies a tiring physical load which has to be carried around whenever the obese person undertakes exercise.

Within the overall though complex and somewhat variable relationship between excessive fatness, exercise and activity there is some specific evidence that sexual activity is reduced amongst subjects. In a controlled study of obese females it was found (Crisp, 1967a) that the former had become significantly less sexually active since the onset of their massive obesity in comparison with non-obese subjects studied over the same period of time. Whilst there were exceptions to this it did appear that at least part of this inactivity was due to the overall increase in inertia. It was suggested that such inertia might sometimes be of psychological importance through its effect of resolving neurotic conflict rooted in ambivalent relationships which had resulted in sexual acting-out behaviour. In this and other studies (Kollar and Atkinson, 1966; Glucksman and coworkers, 1968; Crisp and Stonehill, 1970) it was a clinical observation that some such patients tended to become more sexually active again as they lost weight and as their overall activity levels and confidence grew. Under such circumstances earlier neurotic conflicts of the kind just described were sometimes rekindled.

Overall then there is evidence that links the state of longstanding fatness with disturbances of sleep and daytime activity. Obese subjects tend to sleep longer and to be less active than others. However the picture is a complex and variable one and will also be affected by immediate nutritional factors such as the level of recent food intake as well as by a range of other influences such as drug (including alcohol) intake, occupation and mood.

Mood

A great deal of attention has been directed towards a study of the relationship between mood, especially the disturbances of mood associated with depressive illness, food intake and obesity.

At one level there are those, mainly psychoanalysts, who claim that, during the first six months of life, strong experiential associations can develop between aspects of ingestion and mood (Winnicott, 1958). During this period the infant's inherent nutritional need and sleep/waking pattern, probably already shaped by intra-uterine influences, become interwoven with his sense of security and comfort within his growing relationship with the mother. Such factors as the availability of food, timing of feeds in relation to his rest/activity cycle, the meaning of food to the mother and the admixture of her various feelings towards her dependant infant contribute to this. If the mother overvalues food as some indicator of material security, and has an excessive need for her baby to be seen as well nourished whether within the context of being simply overprotective or else more complicatedly marking her rejecting feelings towards him, then both the perception and ingestion of food may take on additional social meaning for the infant. For instance if food becomes *the* means of placating and rewarding the infant then he may come to overvalue it and thereafter restrict his search for comfort to a concern with it. He may find that a relationship with food is more reassuring and predictable than it is with more complicated 'objects' such as people. This view concerning character development includes such propositions as that the person concerned will tend to eat when lonely, angry or depressed irrespective of his immediate state of 'energy balance' and will thereby gain some comfort. As such a child enters adolescence, already obese and thereafter increasingly self-conscious about his or her appearance, the social withdrawal, avoidance and inactivity already referred to may be compounded by further solitary overeating and yet greater obesity. If such views have any foundation, and whilst it is uncertain as yet as to whether overt depression is more or less common in the obese than in others, it would seem reasonable to propose that such people, deprived of food would be more likely to become depressed than others. However, what evidence there is on the former point is conflicting. For instance Simon (1963) found depression to be reduced amongst a 'healthy' and uncomplaining obese army population compared with a matched non-obese population, and the similar finding revealed by a general population study (Crisp and McGuinness, 1975) was referred to in Chapter 1. There is also a public view of the obese individual as being jolly and confident that dies hard. Such findings and notions appear to conflict with the long-established but now questioned psychiatric proposition that it is the person with pyknic or endomorphic habitus (i.e. the obese like person) who is most likely to develop manic-depressive psychosis. It is however perhaps noteworthy that such an illness would be expected to be associated with a period of reduced food intake and weight loss.

Certainly many authors have reported the development of states of depression as being commonplace amongst obese subjects who are dieting. Both Brüch (1957) and Stunkard (1957) emphasize this in their earlier writings whilst at the same time indicating the pitfalls of concluding that such findings have implications for the causality of obesity. Indeed it is also clear that the majority of people if subjected to food deprivation become miserable, irritable and narrow in their interests (Keys and coworkers, 1950). Meanwhile in 1967 Crisp described the emergence of characterological and interpersonal problems rather than stereotyped psychiatric illness as often occurring in a series of obese patients who had lost substantial amounts of weight, and this again appeared to be the case in a further detailed study of six massively obese patients also losing considerable amounts of weight (Crisp and Stonehill, 1970).

It is not possible then to draw firm conclusions concerning the pattern of mood in obesity. If the majority of obese people eat when depressed or have persistently done so in their past then it would appear that they are different from the majority of depressed people who, it has always been claimed, lose their appetites and eat less under such circumstances. Certainly many obese subjects in the clinic come to acknowledge feelings of great self-consciousness and sometimes associated loneliness, but they are not representative of the obese population at large. Perhaps the term 'depression', which is at the same time both a complex concept and not readily understandable as a mood, is too limiting and superficial a notion for it to be acceptable as being *the* mood relevant to obesity and its determination.

Anorexia Nervosa

Anorexia nervosa is a state of starvation and emaciation associated with avoidance of eating 'fattening' foods. Feeding patterns can range from studious avoidance of nearly all dietary carbohydrate to indiscriminate overeating and related copious vomiting. Many of the features of other kinds of starvation are present e.g. reduced BMR, increased bodily hair, preoccupation with food; but the individual with anorexia nervosa characteristically, and possibly related to her highly selected diet and complex psychological needs, remains wary, alert, energetic and active.

The disorder arises in adolescence usually in females and has been construed as a psychosomatic avoidance response to the maturational psychosocial demands of puberty. It has been described in detail elsewhere (Crisp, 1967b, 1970; Russell, 1970). It is to be considered here in relation to the extraordinary patterns of activity that often accompany it.

Sleep

Individuals with anorexia nervosa are usually concerned to avoid change.

They often conceal their preoccupation with and fears about weight gain from others and are secretive about many aspects of their behaviour. For instance they rarely complain of problems with sleep and usually claim to be sleeping well. Whilst some do sleep for a relatively normal length of time and indeed may occasionally elect to stay in bed as a protection against the temptation to eat, the majority are particularly restless during the second half of the night. After waking initially in the early hours they sleep lightly and finally waken early. At such times as the early morning they may secretly eat or exercise themselves—a practice which is particularly likely to lead them to deny such wakefulness.

Nevertheless, in a study of 60 patients involving careful enquiry and observation Crisp (1967a) found that many were waking before 6.30 a.m. Table 5 shows this in diagrammatic form in relation to other aspects of daytime activity, feeding patterns and mood. There was an impression that the degree of the sleep disorder was proportional to the severity and chronicity of the nutritional disturbance, was more common in those who appeared to be also most aroused during the day (often those habitually overeating and vomiting), and was perhaps less common in those who were sometimes lethargic and sad during the day. It was suggested that such starvation might be re-exposing shorter more primitive rest/activity cycles of a 4-hourly or shorter frequency; furthermore, that such nutritional factors might contribute to the sleep changes in the second half of the night commonly found in a variety of psychiatric and other illnesses.

Activity

The majority of subjects with anorexia nervosa experience a sense of excessive restlessness and vigorously and sometimes ritualistically exercise themselves. Whilst the latter course accords with their wish to lose further weight or at least not gain any, its other basis appears to be more pervasive (see Table 5 again) and to be related to their starved and hyper-aroused state. A general decrease in activity in anorexia nervosa is the exception and once again appears to be related to sadness and fatigue which characterise the occasional person with this disorder.

Mood

The mood of subjects with anorexia nervosa is often highly variable within any one person and certainly within the overall group. In the past this has led clinicians to associate the disorder with one or other of the whole range of psychotic and neurotic disorders. Individuals can swing from experiencing elation together with a sense of ascetism and control to experiencing deep despair and isolation. They often respond irritably and aggressively to those attempting to modify or restrict their eating behaviour and exercise. Their more pervasive feelings may usually be masked by a blandness of manner which accords with their denial of problems. There is little evidence to suggest that such mood states are primary to the presenting disorder; rather do they

Table 5. Clinical data on aspects of activity and sleep in 60 patients with anorexia nervosa. Note the interrupted sleep and early waking (Crisp, 1967a).

Patient No.	Age (yrs)	Compulsive activity		Overall waking activity & restlessness				Major C.O. Fatigue	Overt Depression	Epilepsy	Sleep pattern
		Severe	Marked	Gross over-	Mod. over-	Norm act-	Under act-				
1	14		C		A						
2	17		C		A						
3	23				A						
4	44	C		A							
5	46		C		A						
6	13		C	A				F	D		
7	14		C	A							
8	14	C		A							
9	14		C		A						
10	14	C		A							
11	15		C		A			F			
12	15				A						
13	16		C	A							
14	16		C		A						
15	17		C		A			F			
16	17		C	A				F	D		
17	17			A							
18	17		C		A			F			
19	17	C			A						
20	17		C	A				F	D		
21	18	C			A						
22	18			A							
23	19				A			F	D		
24	19				A					E	
25	19		C	A							
26	19				A						
27	19		C	A							
28	19		C		A						
29	20		C	A				F	D		
30	20				A						
31	20			A							
32	20				A				D		
33	20	C			A			F			
34	20				A				D		
35	21				A						
36	21				A						
37	22		C		A				D	E	
38	23	C		A							
39	27		C		A			F	D	E	
40	28		C		A						
41	29		C		A						
42	29				A					E	
43	29		C		A						
44	29										
45	29				A						
46	29		C		A						
47	30	C		A							
48	33	C		A				F			
49	33				A					E	
50	35	C		A						E	
51	36			A							
52	40	C		A				F	D		
53	42		C		A						
54	42		C		A			F			
55	42		C		A						
56	44		C		A						
57	44		C		A						
58	45		C		A						
59	47		C		A						
60	54		C	A							

Reproduced by kind permission of the Editor, J. Psychosom. Res.

appear to be dependent upon its course and otherwise upon the same underlying neurotic conflicts that are generating it. As already stated the profound disturbances of sleep and activity found in the disorder appear to be more related to the nutritional status than to the mood state.

References

Bloom, W. L. and Eidex, M. F. (1967). Inactivity as a major factor in adult obesity. *Metabolism*, **16**, 679–684.

Brüch, H. (1957). *The Importance of Overweight*, Morton, New York.

Brüch, H. (1964). Psychological aspects of overeating and obesity. *Psychomatics*, **5**, 269–274.

Crisp, A. H. (1967a) The possible significance of some behavioural correlates of weight and carbohydrate intake. *J. Psychosom. Res.*, **11**, 117–131.

Crisp, A. H. (1967b). Anorexia nervosa. *Hosp. Med.*, May, 713–718.

Crisp, A. H. (1970). Anorexia nervosa 'Feeding disorder', 'Nervous malnutrition' or 'Weight phobia'? *World Review of Nutrition and Dietetics*, **12**, 452–504.

Crisp, A. H. and Stonehill, E. (1970). Treatment of obesity with special reference to seven severely obese patients. *J. Psychosom. Res.*, **14**, 327–345.

Crisp, A. H. and McGuinness, B. (1975). Jolly fat, *Br. med. J.*, **4** (In Press).

Glucksman, M. L., Hirsch, J., McCully, R. S., Barron, B. A. and Little, J. L. (1968). The response of obese patients to weight reduction. II. A quantitative evaluation of behaviour. *Psychosom. Med.*, **30**, 1–11.

Keys, A., Brozek, J., Henschel, A., Michelson, O. and Taylor, H. L. (1950). *The Biology of Human Starvation*, Univ. Minnesota Press, Minneapolis.

Kollar, C. and Atkinson, R. (1966). Response of extremely obese patients to starvation. *Psychosom. Med.*, **28**, 227–246.

Mayer, J. (1953). Genetic, traumatic and environmental factors in the pathology of obesity. *Physiol. Rev.*, **33**, 472–508.

Mayer, J. (1964). Appetite and the many obesities. *Aust. Ann. Med.*, **13**, 282–305.

Miller, D. S. and Mumford, P. (1966). Obesity: physical activity and nutrition. *Proc. Nutr. Soc.*, 178th Scientific Symposium, **25(2)**, 100–107.

Parizkova, J. (1968). Nutrition, body fat and physical fitness. *Borden Review of Nutrition Research*, **29**, 41–54.

Russell, G. F. M. (1970). Anorexia Nervosa: Its identity as an illness and its treatment. In Price, J. H. (Ed.), *Modern Trends in Psychological Medicine*. Butterworth, London, pp. 131–164.

Simon, R. I. (1963). Obesity as a depressive equivalent. *J. Am. med. Ass.*, **183**, 208.

Stunkard, A. J. (1957). The dieting depression. *Amer. J. Med.*, **23**, 77–86.

Stunkard, A. J. (1958). Physical activity, emotions and human obesity. *Psychosom. M•d.*, **20**, 366–372.

Winnicott, D. W. (1958). Collected Papers. Tavistock Publications, London, p. 33.

CHAPTER 3

Nutritional and mood disturbances in disorders of sleep

The term disorders of sleep is applied here to embrace a collection of disorders in which sleep disturbance is a prominent feature and in which specific contributory factors such as brain damage are not evident. They include the more pervasive hypersomnias—states of excessive sleepiness—which appear to exist within a number of separate although possibly related syndromes, and also so-called primary narcolepsy, a state distinguished by a more episodic form of daytime somnolence with or without other related symptoms. The insomnias—states of reduced sleep, or if one likes to look at it in the other way, states of undue wakefulness—will also be briefly referred to although they almost always appear to arise as aspects of other syndromes involving mood, nutritional and other disturbances rather than seemingly arising as primary disorders in their own right.

As previously mentioned there is a considerable range of sleep patterns in the general population. Prolonged sleep or daytime episodic sleep is only likely to come to medical attention if it is really excessive or becoming so in relation to the social setting.

Apart from the population studies already referred to, investigation of sleep disturbances has been mainly of the selected groups of patients presenting in the clinic and it is these who have yielded the following syndromes now established in the literature.

Periodic Hypersomnia and Megaphagia

In 1962 Critchley in an authoritative review drew together a number of case reports and added eleven new ones which served to delineate the syndrome. The main clinical features of the disorder are periodic somnolency coupled with increased food and sometimes also fluid intake. Psychological disturbance can be present both immediately before, during and after the attacks which usually last a week or so, sometimes seeming to have started abruptly but more often insidiously with malaise. Sleep may persist throughout the attack apart from spontaneous waking to micturate and defecate and sometimes to eat. If roused the subject is irritable and resentful and quickly falls asleep again unless confronted with food, under which circumstance he usually consumes all that is available. This latter feature, which often involves the ingestion of very large quantities of food, is sometimes subsequently denied by the patient, and Critchley supposed this to be an aspect of his more general 'retrograde amnesia' for the period of the attack. Apart from the preliminary malaise, subjects often showed reactive irritability when wakened from their state of somnolence. Immediately after the episode subjects sometimes reported having had vivid dreams and states of sexual excitement during it, despite their overall hazy recollection of other aspects of their behaviour during the attack. Following the attack individuals were sometimes elated for a short while or else described the experience of depersonalization. Sometimes for a while they appeared muddled in their thinking. Such symptoms disappeared rapidly and in Critchley's judgement the majority of subjects were otherwise unremarkable in their personalities. He goes on to emphasize that the disorder, which had a good prognosis, appeared to arise exclusively in males and almost invariably during adolescence. Although clearly delineating the feature of megaphagia (he did not find that his patients reported an excessive hunger, merely that they ate excessively and indiscriminately when food was available) he did not report obesity to be a common feature of the condition. However, several subjects are said to have subsequently become obese. Furthermore, in drawing upon the previous literature, he noted the similarity between the disorder and the so-called Kleine–Levin syndrome described a decade or two earlier and which is associated with overweight as well as the more specific features outlined by him.

Although Critchley suspected that the disorder was exclusively a male one it is noteworthy that female patients spontaneously gaining weight following or during a phase of anorexia nervosa and within the context of a bout of overeating, may become somnolent and irritable and withdrawn if disturbed. Such a constellation of behaviour may become persistent but more often fluctuates and ultimately remits during the third decade of life. Moreover, more recently several authors (Gilbert, 1964; Duffy and Davison, 1968) have described the established syndrome, as described by Critchley, in females. Perhaps relatedly, and conversely, anorexia nervosa was for long thought to be exclusively a female disorder but this is not the case. It does occur, rarely, in the male. It is therefore of some interest to note the contrast of this adolescent syndrome common in the female of anorexia nervosa, which usually involves food avoidance, hyperactivity and undue wakefulness, with the adolescent syndrome, more common in the male, described by Critchley and with the contrary features of excessive food intake, inactivity and hypersomnia. Psychological states and other aspects of behaviour found by Critchley to be common in this latter condition also overlap with those found in anorexia nervosa patients (Crisp, 1970), e.g. resentment at outside interference, denial of recent experience including excessive food intake, excessive eating in the absence of hunger, episodes of elation and depression, vivid and disturbing dreams following periods of weight gain, depersonalization.

Meanwhile Globus (1969) has recently described a syndrome of fuzzy
thinking and lethargy associated with 'sleeping late', particularly if sleep
lasts for 10 hours or more, whilst Rechtschaffen and Roth (1969) also describe
'post-dormital confusion' in hypersomniacs. Globus speculates that the
phenomena might be related to interference with nutritional/circadian
rhythms. 'Sluggishness' first thing in the day and late rising do often seem
to go together in normal people and one is also reminded of the clinical association between depression, pyknic habitus and morning retardation.

Indeed one is increasingly struck by the overlap between these so-called
primary disorders of sleep and other disorders such as psychiatric disorders.
Thus writers in the latter field have often described syndromes such as
depression which involve weight gain and increased sleep and have also drawn
attention to the way in which hypersomnia sometimes appears to be associated
with an evident need of the individual to withdraw from active life. Under
such circumstances hysterical conversion mechanisms have sometimes been
advanced as the basis for the phenomenon. However such possible links as
these will be referred to in a subsequent chapter.

Meanwhile Critchley was concerned about the possible physiological
mechanisms of the disorder that he had identified. Investigation into aspects
of carbohydrate metabolism were inconclusive but EEG abnormalities do
sometimes arise both between and during attacks (Critchley, 1962; Elian and
Bornstein, 1969; Green and Cracco, 1970). These changes, which appear
to be part of the functional disturbance characteristic of the syndrome have
been viewed as different from those occasionally found in patients, sometimes
older, presenting with symptoms of megaphagia and hypersomnia, which are
either more persistent or progressive and which have been found to be related to
fixed organic cerebral damage based in such pathologies as post-encephalitic
brain damage and cerebral tumours in the region of the third ventricle.

Whilst the above syndrome is of considerable importance in relation to
the theme of this monograph it is in fact a rare one in the clinic, much more
so than the Pickwickian syndrome comprising excessive daytime sleep, obesity
and periodic respiration.

As long ago as 1810, Wadd described 'a country tradesman aged about 30,
of a very short stature and naturally of a fresh sanguine complexion and
very fat . . . . He complained of perpetual drowsiness and inactivity.' The
first modern report of a syndrome of marked obesity, somnolence, cyanosis,
periodic respiration, secondary polycythaemia and pulmonary hypertension
is the description by Sieker and coworkers (1955), and it was Burwell and
coworkers (1956) who again expanded the description and aptly labelled it
the Pickwickian Syndrome (Figure 11). These authors cited the chronic hypoxia
as responsible for the somnolence, whereas Finkelstein and Avery (1963)
believed the narcotic effect of carbon dioxide to be responsible. The latter
authors stated that the syndrome can be found in 10 per cent of massively
obese adults but that it is reversible with weight loss. More recently Hishikawa
and coworkers (1972) have concluded that the daytime hypersomnia is due

Figure 11. The fat boy asleep. Illustration from *The Pickwick
Papers* by Charles Dickens

to the disturbance of nocturnal sleep, compensating for it. Furthermore
that the nocturnal interference with sleep is usually due to the periodic apnoea
consequent on collapse of the pharynx and to which obese subjects are more
prone. Meanwhile Broughton (1972) too has drawn attention to mechanisms
such as specific airway obstruction and posture which can generate both
periodic respiration and hypersomnia or drowsiness in the absence of obesity.
Nevertheless in the clinic massive obesity would appear to remain a common
condition capable of engendering this syndrome, perhaps not only through
its effect of mechanical hindrance to respiration but also its more direct relationship with sleep processes, which are the theme of this book. Bonkalo (1968)
has also drawn attention to the concurrence of sleep disorders and abnormal
food intake in various psychiatric disorders and suggested that this coincidence
could be a direct physiologically determined conjunction of functions. This
view is again contrary to that of Pai (1950) who regarded the association as
being rooted in the complex conversion and avoidance mechanisms of hysteria.

Narcolepsy

Narcolepsy is a term used to describe 'attacks' of relatively sudden, intense
and overwhelming sleep which usually last for a matter of minutes. These
can occur in isolation or may be associated with one or more other symptoms,
the fullest expression of which is the tetrad of narcolepsy, cataplexy, sleep

paralysis and hypnagogic hallucinations. Cataplexy is the commonest other symptom and comprises 'attacks' of sudden loss of postural tone, usually involving the total system and resulting in the subject falling, but sometimes only affecting limited muscle groups. Such attacks are usually preceded by the experience of intense emotions such as laughter or fright. Many people, of course, experience some lesser degree of weakness under such circumstances. Sleep paralysis describes the experience of waking either during sleep onset or from deeper sleep and of being paralysed. The phenomenon is brief in duration. Finally vivid and often unpleasant dreamlike experiences can arise again in the stage of initial sleep onset. They have been called hypnagogic experiences in accord with the use of this term to describe similar experiences which occur more widely in the population.

The tetrad have now been extensively investigated in respect of their cerebral electro-physiological correlates and there is consensus (Broughton, 1972; Roth, Faber and Nevsimalova, 1973) that narcolepsy, when it is the sole sympton, usually takes the form of non-REM slow wave sleep. When other features of the tetrad co-exist then the narcoleptic attack is more commonly associated with REM sleep. Such researchers have concluded that the attacks therefore comprise intrusions of slow wave or REM sleep into normal wake-fulness. Some attempts have been made to relate such episodes to the postulated basic 24-hour rest/activity 90-minute cycle referred to earlier, but the evidence for this is at present patchy. Meanwhile researchers also agree that, when other features of the tetrad are present, then the onset of sleep itself is usually and atypically associated with REM activity. This finding accords with the tendency for such patients to experience paralysis and also dreams (the so-called hypnagogic hallucinations referred to earlier) at this time. However, when narcolepsy is an isolated symptom sleep onset is unremarkable both clinically and in neurophysiological terms in the sense that the EEG sleep stages evolve in the usual way.

The possible physiological mechanisms underlying narcolepsy have been discussed by Hill (1962) and more recently by Broughton and his colleagues (1972) in terms of the functional characteristics of the reticular activating system which is concerned both with arousal and with the motor nerve outflow.

All the features so far described in this chapter are common experience in the sense that many people do experience them to a lesser and less frequent degree than is usually the case with subjects presenting them for help. Our concern is with the ways in which such symptoms arise both within the clinical context and in terms of the more widespread functional integrity of the cerebral regulatory systems.

As previously mentioned, it is clear that the experience of intense emotion often immediately precedes a cataleptic attack. Sours is one of the few psycho-dynamically orientated psychiatrists to take a systematic interest in these disorders, and in 1963 he reported on a large series of patients culled from the records of the Colombia Presbyterian Medical Centre in New York City. Many of them clearly had narcolepsy whilst others had disorders which possibly blended into the other hypersomniac syndromes. Like others he was concerned firstly to separate off those with fixed cerebral pathology, in the main post-encephalitic damage, other brain damage and tumours. Under these latter circumstances the symptoms usually comprised either prolonged hypersomnia or else narcolepsy together with clinical obesity, mood and behavioural disorders such as irritability and sociopathy, and other neurological evidence of specific lesions of the cerebellum and brainstem. His residue of 75 patients with what he called primary narcolepsy showed other characteristics. The mean age of onset was about 18 years and the commonest age of onset was within the second and third decades of life. Abrupt adolescent weight gain, a feature also reported by earlier workers (Cave, 1931; Daniels, 1934; Cutting, 1944), and psychological disturbances were common.

Sours differentiated his narcoleptic patients from those with more prolonged episodes of sleep, stating that attacks usually lasted 10 to 15 minutes whilst subjects usually wakened seemingly refreshed but in fact often remaining rather drowsy for periods between the attacks. In his view the attacks sometimes came on relatively slowly. There was a tendency for the disorder to persist within the subgroup that he was able to follow up, although some few subjects reported remission or diminution of symptoms. He raised the question of whether there is such a phenomenon as primary narcolepsy with or without other features not only of the tetrad of symptoms but also of a psychological kind, and whether it is not always precipitated by some other experiential factor e.g. of a psychological and/or nutritional kind (see also Oswald, 1962). One is reminded in this context of the possibly parallel debates that have gone on concerning such states as idiopathic epilepsy and depersonalization, both of which appear to contain constitutionally determined elements interacting with developmental and more immediate experiential factors.

States of Undue Wakefulness

Very rare cases of prolonged wakefulness have been described in relation to specific cerebral pathology such as brainstem haemorrhages. However, as an aspect of functional cerebral disturbance, wakefulness rarely persists to the extent that somnolence does within the hypersomniac syndrome described above. Patients in severe states of hypomania may remain without sleep for several days before reaching a point of exhaustion, but otherwise undue wakefulness tends to affect the architecture of normal sleep by eroding its onset, interrupting it or hastening its end, rather than by excluding it altogether. Individuals experiencing such wakefulness may complain of it and it is usually called insomnia.

States of mood such as high levels of anxiety, excitement or anger are particularly associated with difficulty in getting off to sleep. States of severe depression are said to be more often associated with early wakening. Such states may also be associated with fragmentation of sleep and are part of the normal range of experience as well as aspects of psychiatric syndromes which will be referred to in more detail later. Episodes of nocturnal wakefulness can also arise in relation to such physiological activities as micturition and the experience of hunger. The extreme degrees of fragmented sleep characteristic of the state of anorexia nervosa have already been described.

References

Bonkalo, A. (1968). Hypersomnia. A discussion of syndrome implications based on three cases. *Brit. J. Psychiat.*, **114**, 69–75.

Broughton, R. (1972). Sleep and clinical pathological states. In Chase, M. H. (Ed.) The Sleeping Brain. *Perceptions in the Brain Sciences*, Vol. 1. Brain Information Service, University of California, Los Angeles.

Burwell, C. S., Robin, E. D. Whale, R. D. and Bickelmann, A. G. (1956). Extreme obesity associated with alveolar hyperventilation—the Pickwickian syndrome. *Amer. J. Med.*, **21**, 811–818.

Cave, H. (1931). Narcolepsy. *Arch. Neurol. Psychiat.*, **26**, 50–101.

Crisp, A. H. (1970). Anorexia nervosa 'Feeding disorder', 'Nervous malnutrition' or Weight phobia'? *World Review of Nutrition and Dietetics*, **12**, 452–504.

Critchley, M. (1962). Periodic hypersomnia and megaphagia in adolescent males. *Brain*, **85**, 627–656.

Cutting, W. C. (1944). Co-existence of obesity and narcolepsy. *Stanford med. Bull.*, **2**, 172–175.

Daniels, L. E. (1934). Narcolepsy. *Medicine, Baltimore*, **13**, 1–122.

Duffy, J. P. and Davison, K. (1968). A female case of the Kleine-Levin syndrome. *Brit. J. Psychiat.*, **114**, 77–84.

Elian, M. and Bornstein, B. (1969). The Kleine–Levin syndrome with intermittent abnormality in the EEG. *Electroencephalogr. Clin. Neurophysiol.*, **27**, 601–604.

Finkelstein, J. W. and Avery, M. E. (1963). The Pickwickian Syndrome. Studies in ventilation and carbohydrate metabolism: case study of a child who recovered. *Amer. J. dis. Child.*, **106**, 251–257.

Gilbert, G. S. (1964). Periodic hypersomnia and bulimia. The Kleine-Levin syndrome. *Neurology, Minneap.*, **14**, 844–850.

Globus, G. G. (1969). A syndrome associated with sleeping late. *Psychosom. Med.*, **31**, 528–535.

Green, L. N. and Cracco, R. Q. (1970). Kleine–Levin syndrome. A case with EEG evidence of periodic brain damage. *Arch. Neurol.*, **22**, 166–175.

Hill, D. (1962). Normal and pathological sleep. *Proc. roy. Soc. Med.*, **55**, 905–907.

Hishikawa, V., Furuya, E., Wakamatsu, H. and Yamamoto, J. (1972) A polygraphic study of hypersomnia with periodic breathing and primary alveolar hypoventilation. *Bull. Psysiopath. Resp.* (Nancy), **8 (5)**, 1139–1151.

Oswald, I. (1962). *Sleeping and Waking*, Elsevier Publ. Co., Amsterdam, pp. 8, 197, 198.

Pai, M. N. (1950). Hypersomnia syndromes. *Brit. med. J.*, **1**, 522–524.

Rechtschaffen, A. and Roth, B. (1969). Nocturnal sleep of hypersomniacs. *Activ. Nerv. Sup.*, **11**, 229–233.

Roth, B., Faber, J. and Nevsimalova, S. (1973). Polygraphic studies in narcolepsy and hypersomnia. In Koella, W. P. and Levin, P. (Eds.) *Sleep*, Karger, Basel, pp. 27–34.

Sieker, H. O., Estes, F. H., Kelsu, G. A. and McIntosh, H. D. (1955). The cardio-pulmonary syndrome associated with extreme obesity. *J. clin. Invest.*, **34**, 916.

Sours, J. A. (1963). Narcolepsy and other disturbances in the sleep–waking rhythm: a study of 115 cases with review of the literature. *J. nerv. ment. Dis.*, **137**, 525–542.

Wadd, W. (1810). Cursory remarks on corpulence: by a member of the Royal College of Surgeons. London.

CHAPTER 4

Sleep, activity and nutrition in psychiatric illness

Although there are wide variations in patterns of sleep, activity and nutrition between individuals, in the adult there is a tendency for a relative stability of pattern within the individual (see Chapter 2). However, temporary fluctuations commonly occur and it is clear that such changes are often severe and frequently described in psychiatric illness. They may occur throughout the range of psychiatric disturbance and may coexist in the individual. However, alterations in sleep patterns, activity and nutritional state, particularly weight change, have traditionally been regarded as prominent features of psychiatric disorders of mood, which include depressive illnesses, mania and anxiety states.

Controversy exists as to whether in terms of aetiology and phenomenology there is more than one type of basic depressive disorder. Work in this area was largely pioneered by the efforts of Kraepelin (1896). He attempted to identify specific psychotic syndromes in terms of their phenomenology and natural histories, thus laying the foundations for treatment evaluation and a search for specific aetiological factors. As a result of his careful observations, he was able to distinguish between the natural history of manic depressive disorder, involutional melancholia and schizophrenia, which he then suggested had different hereditary and constitutional bases. A different view was taken by Freud who stressed the importance of experiential factors and postulated a unitary concept of depression rooted in such matters as the existence of ambivalent relationships and the experience of loss. Popular nosological theories still include unitary, bipolar and multidimensional models of depression (Kiloh and Garside, 1963; Kendell, 1968; Kendell and Gourley, 1970; Eysenck, 1970). Meanwhile emphasis at the present time is placed by many on the multifactorial aetiology of disease embracing genetic, constitutional, experiential and physico-chemical factors.

One of the first clinical descriptions of depression or 'melancholia' is attributed to Hippocrates who drew attention to the association between mood and body build. An early clinical description of an association of disturbed activity, weight and sleep in depression is that of Aretaeus, in the second century A.D. He reported the melancholic patient as 'sad and dismayed. ... They become thin by their agitation and loss of refreshing sleep'. Modern views of the association between the predisposition to psychiatric illness and body build stem largely from the work of Kretschmer (1936). He suggested that pyknic (obese like) individuals showed cyclothymic personality traits and were more liable to manic-depressive psychosis. This is a view that has recently been challenged by the studies of Nicoletti, Magherini and Germanor (1961) and Zerssen, Koellet and Rey (1969).

Nutrition

Attention has been devoted both to changes in appetite and weight in psychiatric illness. There are several reasons for this: changes in appetite and weight are frequent complaints amongst psychiatric patients and cause for concern by their relatives, and they are readily elicited at interview; furthermore, changes in weight during the course of illness have for long been regarded as medically important and they can also be measured easily.

Developments in biochemistry have thrown light on more specific nutritional disturbances in some disorders, for example the role of some vitamin deficiencies in relation to symptomatic psychoses (Spillane, 1947). Disorders of 'nutritional neuropathy' with psychiatric disturbance include pellagra, nicotinic acid deficiency and Wernicke's encephalopathy, but a detailed review of such specific nutritional imbalance is not the aim of this monograph.

Weight changes may occur throughout the range of psychiatric illness, weight loss most commonly being described during the illness with subsequent weight gain on recovery (Post, 1956). Weight gain during illness is not infrequently encountered, often in less severe neurotic illness as well as in association with the consumption of some psychotropic drugs. Such weight changes are usually associated with changes in calorie intake (Duquay and Flach, 1964), but changes in activity and more general energy expenditure also occur in psychiatric illness and a relationship between depression and inactivity which provides a basis for the development of obesity in some individuals has been postulated by Stunkard (1958), and has already been referred to in Chapter 2. Weight change, independent of calorie intake, but related to changes in water metabolism may also occur and have been the subject of investigation in both schizophrenic and affective periodic psychoses (Crammer, 1957).

Weight loss is a common feature of disorders of affect, particularly severe depression and mania, and is also described as an aspect of neurotic disorders, e.g. anxiety phobic states. (Mayer-Gross, Slater and Roth, 1969). Marked weight loss associated with reduction or cessation of calorie intake is common in stuporous states and is of course present in all conditions in which there is refusal to eat or a marked reduction in calorie intake. Such non-specific changes led Bliss and Branch (1960) to coin the phrase 'nervous malnutrition', within which they also included anorexia nervosa but many workers have since challenged the latter proposition (Crisp, 1965; Dally, 1969; Bruch, 1974). Brennan (1945) had found that cases of organic brain disease with mental disturbance showed a statistically significant greater average weight loss than patients in all other diagnostic categories. Amongst this population are many who are unable to care for themselves and weight loss may be one reflection of the inadequacy of those caring for them to meet such patients' basic needs.

Weight gain due to increased calorie intake is generally regarded as less common in association with the development of psychiatric illness, but is sometimes a feature in less severe cases of anxiety state and depressive illness (Pollitt, 1965).

It is concluded that, although weight changes may occur throughout the range of psychiatric illness, the clinician most often pursues inquiry in this direction if he suspects that the patient may be suffering from an affective illness, or else if such weight change, especially weight loss, is the subject of complaint.

Sleep

Sleep disturbance is a common feature in psychiatric illness, most frequently in the form of insomnia but occasionally in the form of hypersomnia. Insomnia is usually classified according to the time of night during which the sleep disturbance is most evident. Thus, the terms 'initial insomnia' and 'early morning waking' are commonly used. Hinton (1962) has emphasized that whilst there is some support for this traditional division, the distinction is by no means clear-cut. In his view it is justifiable to distinguish a group who obtain more sleep in the first part of the night from those who sleep more in the second half of the night. Insomnia has usually been regarded as most evident in disorders of mood (Mayer-Gross, Slater and Roth, 1969) but it may be that depressed patients are more likely than most others to present insomnia as a complaint because of the unpleasant affect associated with wakefulness especially in the early part of the day. A study by Samuel (1964) supports this notion. He used nocturnal motility as a measure of sleep in depressed patients and found that they were able to discriminate between a tranquillizer at night and a placebo, rating sleep more optimistically on the tranquillizer, although the drug did not affect sleep as measured by nocturnal motility. Moreover, the sleep ratings by night nurses observing the patients failed to distinguish the drug from placebo. Kiloh and Garside (1963) found sleep disturbance to be an important factor distinguishing patients diagnosed as suffering from 'endogenous depression' from those diagnosed as suffering from 'neurotic depression'. Those with 'endogenous depression' complained of early morning waking whilst those with 'neurotic depression' showed initial insomnia. Mayer-Gross, Slater and Roth (1969), writing of 'endogenous depression', state: 'Disturbance of sleep is the most important of the bodily symptoms. The patient may have difficulty in getting to sleep but most typically wakes early or several times during the night ... '. They contrast this with 'reactive depression' in which they state: 'Sleep is commonly disturbed, and

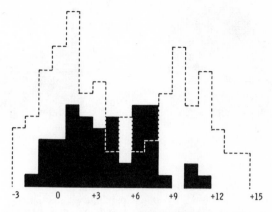

Reproduced by kind permission of
Oxford University Press.

Figure 12. The distributions of 'diagnostic scores'
of two populations of depressed subjects. Scores
were calculated from summation of symptom
loadings, each derived from the relative frequency
of that symptom in the two subpopulations defined
by others as either 'psychotic' or else 'neurotic'.
Maudsley subjects who were unselected depressed
patients nevertheless were found to have a unimodal
distribution of 'diagnostic scores'. The Newcastle
subjects, despite being patients referred for ECT,
displayed a bimodal distribution implying that
there are two discrete categories of depression.
(Kendell, 1968) Both studies have been criticized
on methodological grounds

may be interrupted by unpleasant dreams. But a particular tendency to waking
early in the morning is unusual ...'. A number of other experimental studies
support the association of early morning waking with the diagnosis of 'endogenous depression' and use these findings to support a belief that 'endogenous
depression' and 'neurotic depression' are discrete and separate disorders.
The methodology of Kiloh and Garside (1963) has been criticized by
McConaghy, Joffe and Murphy (1967) and their replication of the former
study did not support the evidence in favour of the independent existence of
'neurotic' and 'endogenous' depressions, and this result is akin to the finding
of Kendell (1968) (Figure 12).

Other studies have also failed to distinguish between the sleep patterns in
'endogenous' and 'neurotic' depression and their findings support the view
that there is a continuum from mild to severe depression embracing the features
of neurotic and endogenous depression. These studies include the work of
Hinton (1963) and Costello and Selby (1965) (see Figure 13).

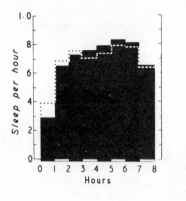
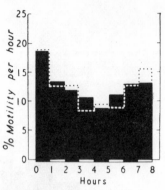

Reproduced by kind permission of the Editor,
J. Neurol. Neurosurg. Psychiat.

Figure 13. Distribution of sleep and standardized motility scores
of patients diagnosed by other psychiatrists as having either
endogenous (solid black) or reactive depression (broken line).
Duration of sleep per hour based on nurse observations. Motility
measured by motility bed (Hinton, 1963)

Evidence from continuous all-night electroencephalograph recordings
in 'endogenous' depression suggest that wakefulness occurs throughout the
night (Oswald and coworkers, 1963). Furthermore, in an EEG study of 21
patients with a variety of types of depression, Hawkins and Mendels (1966)
failed to distinguish patterns of sleep disturbance differentiating the types.
In comparison with a control group of 15 subjects they found that depressed
patients were characterized by delay in sleep onset, decreased total amount of
sleep, frequent waking throughout the night and earlier time of final waking.
The greatest amount of wakefulness occurred during the last third of the night.
They suggested that the pattern of sleep disturbance is more likely to be related
to the severity of the depression rather than to a specific type. In spite of the
nosological controversy referred to above it may be concluded from the
existing literature that patients with severe depression are likely to sleep
particularly poorly in the last third of the night and to complain of early
morning waking.

There is also evidence that sleep disturbance, including early morning waking,
is a feature in psychiatric disturbance other than the affective disorders.
McGhie (1966) obtained data on sleep patterns from a questionnaire given
to 400 consecutive mental hospital admissions. He found that the patient
group slept less well than a normal population from a previous study (McGhie
and Russell, 1962) referred to in Chapter 1 (Figures 14 and 15).

The highest prevalence of overall sleep disturbance was in the neurotic,
psychopathic and alcoholic groups. The depressive group had less overall
sleep disturbance and the organic, paranoid and schizophrenic groups least
disturbance (Figure 16).

Seventeen per cent of all patients suffered from early morning waking

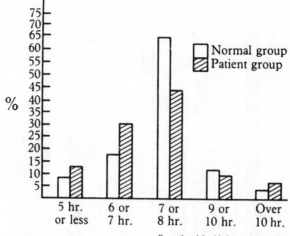

Figure 14. Distribution of total sleep period. Forty-two per cent of psychiatric in-patients reported below average sleep period compared with 23 per cent of the normal sample (McGhie, 1966)

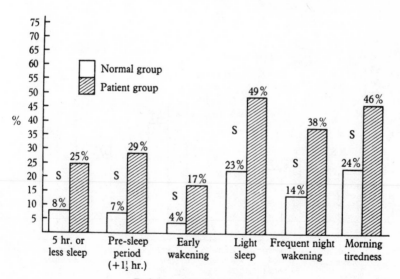

Patient *v.* normal group comparison.

Figure 15. Comparison of psychiatric in-patients and normal subjects in terms of a variety of reported sleep characteristics. The differences between the two groups on each of the six variables are significant beyond the one per cent level (McGhie, 1966)

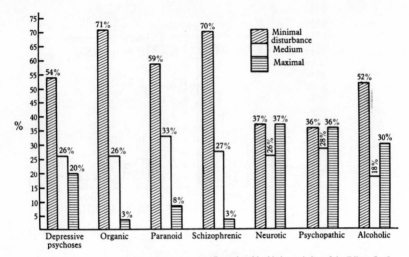

Reproduced by kind permission of the Editor, *Br. J. med. Psychol.*

Figure 16. Overall sleep disturbances reported by psychiatric patients in relation to diagnostic categories (McGhie, 1966)

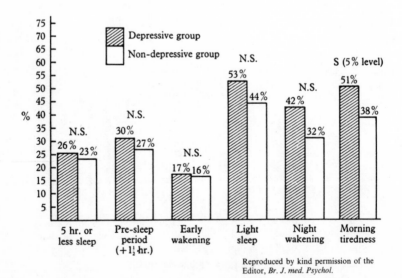

Reproduced by kind permission of the Editor, *Br. J. med. Psychol.*

Figure 17. Self-reported sleep characteristics of psychiatric in-patients examined in relation to whether or not they have been diagnosed as having 'affective' psychosis (McGhie, 1966)

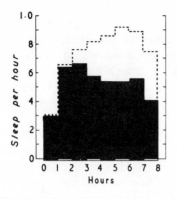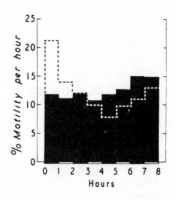

Figure 18. Distribution of sleep and standardized motility scores of patients diagnosed by other psychiatrists as having depressive illness with agitation (solid black) or without (broken line) (Hinton, 1963)

(defined as waking before 5.0 a.m.) compared with 4 per cent of the normal population. There was a similar prevalence of early morning waking in patients diagnosed as depressed as in the non-depressives (Figure 17).

A more detailed questionnaire given to 30 depressed patients revealed that 5 out of the 6 in this group who had early morning waking suffered from agitation and restlessness. This latter observation supports the finding of Hinton (1963) wherein clinically observable agitation (purposeless restlessness) was strongly associated with a greater loss of sleep in the latter part of the night (Figure 18).

Other studies have supported the finding that sleep disturbance is common in psychiatric illness other than depressive disorder. Willis (1965) examined the night nurses' sleep charts on 129 in-patients in the psychiatric department of Guy's Hospital, London. He also found that sleep disturbance was a feature in all diagnostic categories and that those patients with organic brain syndromes had the highest level of all-round wakefulness. Early morning waking was a feature of all groups except the schizophrenics and sleep disturbance tended to improve during hospitalization. Ward (1968) also found sleep disturbance to be a general feature of females admitted to a psychiatric ward. He investigated 87 women and nearly two-thirds of these complained of shortness of sleep time. Similar findings were reported by Detre (1966) who found sleep disturbance to be present in 70 per cent of 295 newly admitted psychiatric patients with a variety of diagnoses. It may be concluded that sleep disturbance is as common a feature in non-depressed psychiatric patients as in depressed psychiatric patients but patients with depressive illness may complain more of such sleep disturbance because of the unpleasantness of wakefulness particularly in the morning.

Activity

Disturbance in the direction of either increased or reduced musculo-skeletal activity often occurs in psychiatric illness. It is evident that amongst animals threat can produce either immobility, active attack behaviour or else escape through flight. It has been argued that immobility under such circumstances may reflect a learned unresponsivity to painful stimuli, a need to maintain bodily control in the face of threatened disintegration or the advantage of being less conspicuous, and that it may also have 'social' values, maintaining the integrity of the herd and also its heirarchical structure in the face of either external or internal challenge, and attempts have been made to interpret the motor disturbances associated with depression in humans in similar terms (Price, 1967).

Qualitative changes in musculo-skeletal activity commonly occur in psychiatric illness in the form of ticks, tremors etc. Structural damage to the brain, especially in the region of the basal ganglia may also, of course, be associated with hyperkinetic syndromes such as chorea and athetosis or hypokinetic disorders such as Parkinson's disease. However this section limits itself to a discussion of quantitative changes in activity in psychiatric illness.

Alternations in activity accompany sleep disturbance. Generally, nocturnal motility has been shown to bear a reciprocal relation with the depth of sleep as measured by the electroencephalogram (Loomis, Harvey and Hobart, 1937) and nocturnal motility has been used as an indicator of the amount and depth of sleep. Although differences in inter-individual nocturnal motility patterns are great, and may exceed intra-individual changes due to illness (Hinton, 1963), if the individual sleep pattern is unchanged then his nocturnal motility pattern usually remains fairly consistent.

Alterations in psychomotor activity during the day frequently occur in psychiatric illness. Restlessness and agitation is not specific to any diagnosis and may occur in any syndrome. It is often an accompaniment of severe anxiety and is particularly evident in frank anxiety states and in depressive illness in which anxiety is a feature. Increased motor activity may also be a feature in any psychosis, especially in those of acute onset such as toxic confusional states, but it is also to be found in some gradually dementing patients. It also occurs in functional psychoses, and in schizophrenia may be seen in an extreme form in catatonic excitement. Perhaps most commonly it is reported as a feature in affective psychoses, especially so-called 'agitated depression' and in mania. Both Hinton and McGhie independently showed that the agitated group of depressed patients displayed most significant early morning waking. Disturbances in activity may fluctuate in the individual during the day. Reduction in activity is seen in its most marked form in stupor which may occur in depressive, schizophrenic or hysterical syndromes. Psychomotor retardation on the other hand is also often a feature of severe depressive illness and frequently displays a marked diurnal variation with most reduction of activity in the morning.

Sleep and Weight Changes in Depression

Finally an association between sleep disturbance and weight change has been reported as being a common feature of depressive illness. Hypersomnia occasionally occurs and Michaelis (1964) has described the association of hypersomnia and increased appetite in depression. However, the coexistence of insomnia and weight loss is more common and they are regarded by many as 'endogenous' features. Carney, Roth and Garside (1965) rated 129 in-patients with depressive illness on 35 items including the presence of early morning waking and weight loss. Intercorrelations between the features were computed and the correlation between early morning waking and weight loss was 0.23 which is statistically significant. Items were extracted predicting a good ECT response in such depressive patients and these items included the presence of both weight loss and early morning waking. A similar study but based on depressed out-patients was carried out by Kiloh and Garside (1963) and their findings also revealed a significant correlation between weight loss and early morning waking. Other studies have also shown such an association. Pichot and Lampérière (1964) administered a questionnaire to 135 depressed patients and showed loss of appetite, weight loss and insomnia to be associated. Beck (1967) in a study of 606 depressed patients produced similar findings.

As already indicated the clustering of symptoms in depression is taken by some authors (Kiloh and Garside, 1963; Carney, Roth and Garside, 1965) to provide support for the notion of the independent existence of 'neurotic' and 'endogenous' depression. However, none of the studies quoted suggests a causal link between weight loss and insomnia but by inference regard these features as being solely integral aspects of a biological factor which is also promoting the disturbed mood.

The possible relationship between sleep, activity and nutrition in psychiatric illness is clearly complex. Such complexity is contributed to by the difficulties in evaluating any single vegetative component which itself may also have complex origins. To take an example from another aspect of psychiatric illness, constipation is often a complaint in depressed patients. Reduction in food intake as a result of depressive loss of appetite may contribute directly to its presence, but vegetative phenomena associated with other aspects of the disturbed nutritional status and the mental state may also play a part. In addition alteration in psychomotor activity, commonly present in depression and often varying with time of day, may affect intestinal motility which may yet be further influenced by antidepressant medication. These interacting factors may also be compounded by perceptual distortion of the experience by the patient.

References

Aretaeus (c. 150 A. D.) The extant work of Aretaeus, the Cappadocian. Ed. and trans. by Adams, F. Sydenham Soc., London. pubd. 1856.

Beck, A. T. (1967). *Depression. Clinical, experimental and theoretical aspects*, Staples Press, London, pp 33–34.

Bliss, E. L. and Branch, C. H. H. (1960). *Anorexia nervosa*, Paul B. Hoeber Inc., New York:

Brenan, E. L. (1945). Metabolic facets in psychiatric problems. *Dig. Neurol. Psychiat. Inst. of Living*, **13**, 542.

Bruch, H. (1974). *Eating disorders*, Routledge and Kegan Paul, London.

Carney, M. W. P., Roth, M. and Garside, R. F. (1965). The diagnosis of depressive syndromes and the prediction of ECT response. *Brit. J. Psychiat.*, **111**, 659–674.

Costello, C. G. and Selby, M. M. (1965). The relationship between sleep patterns and reactive and endogenous depression. *Brit. J. Psychiat.*, **111**, 497–501.

Crammer, J. L. (1957). Rapid weight changes in mental patients. *Lancet*, **2**, 259–262.

Crisp, A. H. (1965). Some aspects of the evolution, presentation and follow-up of anorexia nervosa. *Proc. Roy. Soc. Med.*, **58**, 814–820.

Dally, P. (1969). *Anorexia nervosa*, Heinemann, London.

Detre, T. (1966). The depressive group of illnesses: sleep disorder and psychoses. *Cen. Psych. Ass. J.*, **2**, (Suppl.), 169–177.

Duquay, R. and Flach, F. F. (1964). An experimental study of weight changes in depression. *Acta. Psychiat. Scand.*, **40**, 1–9.

Eysenck, H. J. (1970). The classification of depressive illness. *Brit. J. Psychiat.*, **117**, 241–250.

Freud, S. (1955). *Mourning and melancholia*, Hogarth Press, London.

Hawkins, D. R. and Mendels, J. (1966). Sleep disturbance in depressive syndromes. *Amer. J. Psychiat.*, **123**, 682–690.

Hinton, J. M. (1962). Sleep and motility in depressive illness. *Proc. Roy. Soc. Med.*, **55**, 907–910.

Hinton, J. M. (1963). Patterns of insomnia in depressive states. *J. neurol. Neurosurg. Psychiat.*, **26**, 184–189.

Kendell, R. E. (1968). *The classification of depressive illness*, Maudsley Monograph No. 18. Oxford University Press, Oxford.

Kendell, R. E. and Gourley, J. (1970). The clinical distinction between psychotic and neurotic depressions. *Brit. J. Psychiat.*, **117**, 257–266.

Kiloh, L. G. and Garside, R. F. (1963). The independence of neurotic depression and endogenous depression. *Brit. J. Psychiat.*, **109**, 451–463.

Kraepelin, E. (1896). *Psychiatrie* (5th Edition), Bartt, Leipzig.

Kretschmer, E. (1936) *Physique and character*, 2nd Edition, revised E. Miller. Kegan Paul, London.

Loomis, A. L., Harvey, E. N. and Hobart, G. A. (1937). Cerebral states during sleep as studied by human brain potentials. *J. exper. Psychol.*, **21**, 127–144.

Mayer-Gross, W., Slater, E. and Roth, M. (1969). *Clinical Psychiatry*, Slater E. and Roth M. (Eds.) Bailliere, Tindall and Cassell, London.

McConaghy, N., Joffe, A. D. and Murphy, B. (1967). The independence of neurotic and endogenous depression. *Brit. J. Psychiat.*, **113**, 479–484.

McGhie, A. (1966). The subjective assessment of sleep patterns in psychiatric illness. *Brit. J. med. Psychol.*, **39**, 221–230.

McGhie, A. and Russell, S. M. (1962). Subjective sleep disturbance in the normal population. *J. ment. Sci.*, **108**, 642–654.

Michaelis, R. (1964). Depressive verstimmung und schlafsucht. *Arch. Pysch. NervKrankh.*, **206**, 345–355.

Nicoletti, I., Magherini, G. and Germano, G. (1961). Richerche fattoriali sulla tipologia morfologica nella psicosi maniaco-depressiva comparativamente. *Riv. Neurobiol.*, **1**, 3.

Oswald, I., Berger, R. J., Jamarillo, R. A., Keddie, K. M. G., Olley, P. G. and Plunkett, G. B. (1963). Melancholia and barbiturates: a controlled EEG body and eye movement study of sleep. *Brit. J. Psychiat.*, **109**, 66–78.

Pichot, P. and Lampérière, T. (1964) Analyse factorielle d'un questionnaire d'auto-évaluation des symptoms depressifs. *Rev. Psychol. Appl.*, **15**, 15–29.

Pollitt, J. (1965). *Depression and its treatment*, William Heinemann Medical Books, London.

Post, F. (1956). Body changes in psychiatric illness: A critical survey of the literature. *J. Psychosom. Res.*, **1**, 219–226.

Price, J. S. (1967). The dominance heirarchy and evolution of mental illness. *Lancet*, **2**, 243–246.

Samuel, J. G. (1964). Sleep disturbance in depressed patients: objective and subjective measures. *Brit. J. Psychiat.*, **110**, 711–719.

Spillane, J. D. (1947). Nutrition of disorders of the nervous system. Livingstone, Edinburgh.

Stunkard, A. J. (1958). Physical activity, emotions and human obesity. *Psychosom. Med.*, **20**, 366–372.

Ward, J. A. (1968). Alterations of sleep patterns in psychiatric disorder. *Cen. Psych. Ass. J.*, **13**, 249–257.

Willis, J. H. P. (1965). Insomnia in psychiatric patients. *Guy's Hosp. Rep.*, **114**, 249–255.

Zersen, D., Koeller, D. M. and Rey, E. R. (1969). Objectivierende untersuchungen zur prämorbiden persönlichkeit endogen depressiver. In Hippins, H. and Selbach, H. (Eds.) *Das depressive syndrom*, Urban und Schwarzenberg, München, pp. 183–205.

CHAPTER 5

Relationship between sleep, activity and nutritional status: experimental literature

Disturbances of appetite and weight are common with lesions in the brain near the ventromedial nucleus of the hypothalamus (Anand and Broback, 1951), and the presence of both 'feeding' and 'satiety' centres is established in many species (Ganong, 1963). Although there has been much speculation over the existence of a 'sleep centre' there is little evidence in favour of the existence of a discrete site of such a centre. However, lesions in the hypothalamus (Oswald, 1962), and particularly the periventricular grey matter and adjacent portions of the aqueduct (Kleitman, 1963), can induce somnolence and are often associated with weight gain and reduced activity.

Meanwhile it is a common belief based on our own personal experience and from the observation of our children and pets, that drowsiness and sleep may follow and be promoted by a meal. Conversely alertness and restlessness are often associated with hunger.

The experimental literature in this field is mainly concerned with the manipulation of nutritional intake and the effect of this on sleep and activity. Such work has been carried out both with animals and humans, and there are reports in the literature of the impact of the effects of starvation in natural famine conditions and in prisoner-of-war concentration camps on sleep and activity.

Animal Literature

Ethological studies support the view that food deprivation is associated with restlessness and food seeking behaviour whilst satiation is associated with inactivity. However there are clearly many other factors which can also either promote sleep, delay its onset or otherwise interfere with the sleep process. For instance quietness and darkness are conducive to sleep but bodily discomfort, light and noise tend to disturb sleep. Diminution of sensory stimulation is conducive to sleep. Thus, if in experimental animals the senses of sight, hearing and smell are oblated then such animals sleep most of the time. Hagamen (1959) reported that 10 blind, deaf and anosmic cats which usually slept nearly all the time, slept much less when fasted. Although this experiment showed that food deprivation may affect the sleep/wakefulness cycle, Folk (1954) showed that light/dark reversal is a more powerful factor than a change in feeding schedule in causing the activity rhythm of rodents to become inverted. Indeed, the 24-hour activity cycle has been related most closely to light and darkness. However Lehmkuhl (1935) showed that in pigeons hunger could have an impact upon this cycle. The experimental literature concerning the impact of hunger on sleep and activity is not, however, conclusive, for Kleitman and Camille (1932) reported no marked increase in the motility of decorticated dogs when it was expected that they would be hungry, but they did show a temporary decrease in activity following feeding. Anokhin (1961) conducted an electro-physiological study of the arousal status of cats. He showed that when food was passed directly by tube to the stomach and glucose administered intravenously, then the EEG arousal pattern promptly gave way to a record of pronounced synchrony in both cortical and hypothalamic channels.

There is a considerable experimental literature describing the relationship between food deprivation and activity in the rat. Treichler and Hall (1962) compared 60 food-deprived rats with 15 controls. Activity was measured by an activity wheel and was shown to increase up to 200 per cent at 90 per cent body weight; 600 per cent at 75 per cent body weight; 700 per cent at 70 per cent body weight and 1400 per cent at 60 per cent body weight. Another study by Moscowitz (1959) reported that activity, again measured by the activity wheel, in rats deprived of food and water did not increase until the rats had lost between 5 and 10 per cent of their body weight. Clearly, physical weakness as a result of food deprivation is a factor which is likely to affect activity, and Wald and Jackson (1944) found that although rats increased their running activity several times if they were deprived of food and water, after 4 days such activity decreased owing to weakness. Other control studies have supported the association between food deprivation and increased activity. Siegel and Steinberg (1949) measured the activity of male albino rats by means of a photo-electric recording device in the cage. During a control period of ad lib feeding and watering the mean half-hourly activity score for the 60 rats was 16.8. After 12, 24, 36 and 48 hours deprivation activity scores had risen to 29.0, 36.1, 36.5 and 39.3 respectively. Similarly, Bolles (1963) allowed experimental rats ad lib feeding for two weeks to establish a baseline of activity. He then divided the sample into deprived and control groups, the deprived group being fed only once every 24 hours. During 12 days deprivation, body weight of the experimental group fell by 15 to 20 per cent. Observations of activity were made hourly and on day 9 of deprivation, both resting behaviour and activity had significantly decreased, and there was a trend in the direction of reduced sleep. In contrast to Wald and Jackson's experiment of total starvation, this latter experiment was of semi-starvation only and thus weight loss was not so rapid or severe and physical weakness did not supervene at such an early stage. Other studies including those of Richter (1927), Shirley (1928), Warner (1928) and Skinner (1936) have shown that in the observation of experimental animals activity increases in the time preceding feeding.

It may be concluded from the animal literature, therefore, that there is a clear association between food deprivation and increased activity and decreased sleep as well as between satiety and rest, but this relationship is likely to be affected by other variables such as lightness and darkness and the effect of physical weakness following total starvation.

Human Experimental Literature

Unlike the animal literature, the human experimental literature concerning the relationship between sleep and nutrition is conflicting.

The literature relating sleep, activity and nutrition in infants generally supports the findings in the animal experimental literature. Thus, Nielsen and Sedgwick (1949) described an anencephalic infant with no intact anatomical structures higher than the mesencephalic level. The infant lived for 85 days and slept after feeding but awakened when hungry. Irwin (1932), Marquis (1941), and Moore and Ucko (1957) independently described the activity of neonates on a 3 to 4-hour fixed feeding schedule. They observed a marked increase in activity towards the end of the interfeeding period. Kleitman (1963) reported that although the 50-60 minute rest/activity cycle of the neonate soon becomes coupled with the 3 to 4-hour gastric cycle, it later becomes modified by daily astronomical and social periodicity, eventually becoming a 24-hour rhythm (Figure 19).

There have been a number of reports of the effect of food eaten during the day on the immediate night's sleep. Stanley and Tescher (1932) reported that more restful sleep can be obtained if nothing is eaten before going to bed, and Rice (1931) and Giddings (1934) ascribed restlessness during sleep not so much to undereating but to overeating, and these findings are in contrast to the evidence from animal experiments. In an experimental study of hunger and its relation to activity, Wada (1922) reported that body movements during sleep occurred simultaneously with stomach contractions. Hamilton, Callahan and Kelly (1966) attempted to measure the effect of a bedtime snack on nocturnal motility. Thirty-six male subjects, living in an institutional environment, slept for an average of 20 nights each on beds which mechanically recorded the movement of the bedsprings throughout the night. There was no dietary control throughout the day but on approximately half the nights each subject consumed a 275-calorie cereal snack at bedtime. The authors reported no difference between nocturnal motility recorded with and without the bedtime snack. The experiment can be criticized for its poor design and for the insensitivity of the measuring device.

A similar experiment was carried out by Laird and Drexel (1934), who measured nocturnal motility in eight adults and eight children on a normal diet. On some nights a bedtime snack of 'easy to digest' food (cornflakes) was given, and on some nights a bedtime snack of 'hard to digest' food (containing hemicellulose), and on other nights no bedtime snack was given. They found 6 per cent less motility on the nights following the 'easy to digest' food

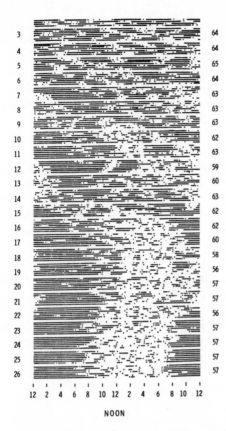

Figure 19 Chart showing the development over the first six months of life of a 24-hour sleep/wakefulness rhythm in a female infant on a free demand sleep/wakefulness rhythm and feeding schedule. Each line represents a 24-hour calendar day. The lines are sleep periods, measured to the nearest 5 minutes; the breaks in the lines wakefulness; the dots feedings. Each group of seven lines is separated from adjacent groups by a double spot. The weeks are indicated on the left; percentage of time spent in sleep during the successive weeks on the right; time in 2-hourly intervals at the bottom (Kleitman, 1963)

compared with the nights on which no snack was taken. Conversely, nocturnal motility was 6 per cent greater following the 'hard to digest' snack than when no snack was taken. They suggested that hunger pangs increase arousal and that a suitable bedtime snack can delay hunger pangs promoting better sleep. Similar findings were reported by Maliniak (1934) who observed that although fasting had a calming effect on the first night's motility, it had a disturbing effect on subsequent nights. Keys and coworkers (1950) in their detailed study on the biology of human starvation measured nocturnal motility during experimental semi-starvation in 9 subjects in the course of the well-known Minnesota experiment, which was designed to measure many physical and psychological effects of starvation. Measurements were made during months 1, 3 and 5 of the experiment and results revealed no significant intra-subject difference in the motility scores. Althouth the authors do not describe full experimental details in their book, the study may be criticized for its lack of a pre-starvation control experimental period and for the insensitivity of the device recording the movement of the bedsprings. Recently two experiments have described the effect of a hot bedtime milk cereal drink on nocturnal motility and sleep. Southwell, Evans and Hunt (1972) used time-lapse cinematography taking one frame every 15 seconds to record body movement throughout

48

the night in four male medical students. There were three experimental conditions: before going to bed each student either had no drink or 350 ml. of warm water or 350 ml. of milk with Horlicks (a cereal milk drink) added. Each subject slept between 3 and 12 times under these conditions before the results were recorded in order to habituate to the experimental circumstances. Recordings were then made twice in each subject under each of the three experimental conditions and results were analysed for recordings between 1.0 a.m. and 7.0 a.m. Although there was no difference in the three experimental conditions in the amount and number of large body movements, there was a significant diminution in small movements after Horlicks in milk and this was particularly marked in the second half of the recording period (Figure 20). A study by Brezinova and Oswald (1972) compared the effect of Horlicks in hot milk with an inert yellow capsule on sleep as measured by the continuous all-night electroencephalogram. Subjects were divided into two age groups. There were 10 healthy young volunteers (6 males and 4 females) with a mean age of 22 years and 8 healthy volunteers with a mean age of 55 years (3 males and 5 females). Each subject slept in a sleep laboratory for 10 nights spread over a period of a few weeks, and before going to bed received either an inert capsule or a drink of Horlicks in milk. The first two nights were treated as adaptation nights and the results discarded. As in the study described above, restlessness during sleep was diminished after Horlicks in the young group of 10 subjects

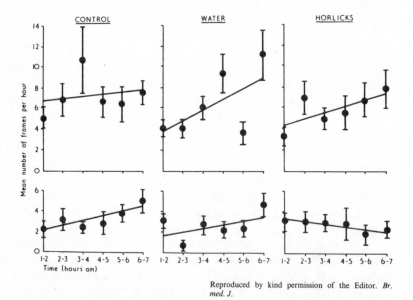

Reproduced by kind permission of the Editor. *Br. med. J.*

Figure 20. Effects of water and Horlicks on movement during sleep. The top charts refer to big movements (e.g. of trunk); the bottom charts to small movements (e.g. hand, foot, head). The lines were fitted by the method of least squares (Southwell, Evans and Hunt, 1972)

and this was most marked in the last three hours of recording. No other features of sleep showed significant differences in this group of subjects. However in the older age group the mean duration of sleep was prolonged after Horlicks in milk and furthermore although the advantage of Horlicks in milk was present throughout the night, it was most marked in the second half of the night. In this group it was also found that the advantage of Horlicks in milk became more marked after repeated administration over a number of nights (Figure 21).

It is possible to criticize these studies as they were not conducted blind. That is to say the experimental subjects knew whether they had taken a milk cereal drink or not and the effect of suggestion might have influenced their sleep and motility. If this were the case it is more likely that the effect would be most evident at the beginning of the night, and this was not so.

There are a number of reports in the literature of sleep and activity characteristics during severe starvation. These studies, usually anecdotal in character, are mainly descriptions of concentration camp survivors and famine victims. Interpretation of these reports is difficult on two grounds. Firstly the subjects are in a situation of great stress and, although evidently starving, clearly their emotional state is a factor which may also have had a

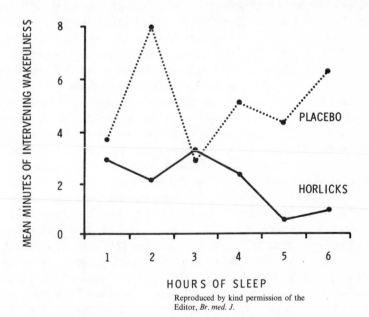

HOURS OF SLEEP

Reproduced by kind permission of the
Editor, *Br. med. J.*

Figure 21. Sleep of older people after placebo or Horlicks. Sleep was significantly less broken after bedtime Horlicks ($p < 0.02$). Successive completed hours of sleep are shown, each point being based on 32 placebo and 32 Horlicks nights (Brezinova and Oswald, 1972)

profound influence on their sleep. Secondly, in severe starvation, physical weakness is likely to give rise to reduced activity and finally collapse. One of the early descriptions is that of Howard in 1839 reporting the manifestations of starvation amongst the destitute poor. In spite of the presence of languor and exhaustion he reported evidence of arousal 'a highly nervous state; he is startled by any sudden noise'. Certainly restlessness is absent from descriptions of terminal starvation. Lipscomb (1945) described the clinical state of the survivors of Belsen, of whom about 20 per cent were dying at the time of its liberation. Reduction in activity sometimes reaching complete immobility was a striking feature. Hottiger and coworkers (1948) also described the presence of drowsiness in a similar population and Hassin (1924), writing of the Russian famine of 1918 to 1922, described apathy, somnolence and immobility in the late stages of starvation. Other reports include those of Leyton (1946), a captured medical officer, who made observations of the effects of slow starvation on subjects in German prisoner-of-war camps during the Second World War. He described apathy and somnolence, the number of hours spent in bed rising from a normal 8 to 16 or more per day. There are other reports, however, perhaps of less severely starving populations, in which physical exhaustion is not a feature, but in which restlessness is described. Blanton (1919) observed children suffering from under-nutrition in the 1914–1918 war. Although they lacked endurance and required more sleep at night, teachers reported restlessness by day. Russell Davis (1951) described the clinical effects of under-nutrition in post-war Germany. As well as such classical features of under-nutrition as fatigue and weakness, restlessness and irritability were found to be characteristic. Insomnia, particularly in the middle and second half of the night, was also a striking feature affecting as many as 50 per cent of subjects. This author suggested that these symptoms were likely to have been 'emotionally' rather than 'physically' determined.

The conclusions then from the animal experimental literature seem to be clear. An association is evident between weight loss and increased activity, whilst restlessness is evident in the prefeeding periods. Human experimental studies are less conclusive. Some of the earlier studies failed to show an association between dietary manipulation and motility during the subsequent night's sleep, but many of these studies may be criticized on methodological grounds both in terms of general design and insensitivity of experimental apparatus. More recent studies, and particularly those of Southwell, Evans and Hunt (1972) and Brezinova and Oswald (1972) clearly support the notion of an immediate link between nutritional status, nocturnal motility and sleep. The human starvation literature is conflicting and difficult to interpret. Overall it may be concluded that there is good experimental evidence supporting a link between nutrition and activity and sleep. In teleological terms the activity of the hungry animal may be construed as adaptive in relation to its search for food, and rest associated with satiety as the state most conducive to bodily anabolic processes.

References

Anand, B. K. and Broback, J. R. (1951). Hypothalamic control of food intake in rats and cats. *Yale J. biol. Med.*, **24**, 123–129.

Anokhin, P. K. (1961). The multiple ascending influences of the subcortical centres on the cerebral cortex. In Brazier, M. A. B. (Ed.), *Brain and Behaviour*, Vol. 1. Amer. Inst. biol. Sciences, Washington, p. 156.

Blanton, S. (1919). Mental and nervous changes in children of the Volkschulen of Trier, Germany, caused by malnutrition. *Ment. Hyg.*, Lond., **3**, 343–386.

Bolles, A. C. (1963). Effect of food deprivation upon the rat's behaviour in its home cage. *J. comp. physiol. Psychol.*, **56**, 456–460.

Brezinova, V. and Oswald, I. (1972). Sleep after a bedtime beverage. *Brit. med. J.*, **2**, 431–433.

Folk, G. E., Jr. (1954). The effect of restricted feeding time on the diurnal rhythm of running activity in the white rat. *Anat. Rec.*, **120**, 786–787.

Ganong, W. F. (1963). *Review of Medical Psychology*, Longe Medical Publications, Los Angeles, p. 161.

Giddings, G. (1934). Child's sleep: effect of certain foods and beverages on sleep motility. *Amer. J. pub. Hlth.*, **24**, 609–614.

Hagamen, W. D. (1959). Responses of cats to tactile and noxious stimuli. *A. M. A. Archs. Neurol.*, **1**, 203–215.

Hamilton, L. H., Callahan, R. and Kelly, F. P. (1966). Effect of a bedtime snack on sleep. *J. Amer. diet. Ass.*, **48**, 395–398.

Hassin, G. B. (1924). Brain changes in starvation. *Arch. neurol. Psychiat.*, **11**, 551–556.

Hottiger, A., Gsell, O., Vehinger, E., Salzmann, C. and Labhardt, A. (1948). *Hungerkrankheit, Hungeröden, Hungertuberkulose*, Benno Schwalbe, Basel, p. 126.

Howard, R. B. (1839). *An inquiry into the morbid effect of deficiency of food chiefly with reference to their occurrence amongst the destitute poor.* Simpkin, Marshall and Co., London, p. 27.

Irwin, O. C. (1932). The amount of motility in 73 new-born infants. *J. comp. Psychol.*, **14**, 415–428.

Keys, A., Brozek, J., Henschel, A. Mickelson, Q. and Taylor, H. L. (1950). *The Biology of Human Starvation*, Vol. 1, Univ. Minnesota Press., Minneapolis, pp. 700–701.

Kleitman, N. (1963). *Sleep and Wakefulness*, Univ. Chicago Press, Chicago, pp. 132–133; 262–273.

Kleitman, N. and Cammille, N. (1932). Studies on the physiology of sleep. VI. Behaviour of decorticated dogs. *Amer. J. Psysiol.*, **100**, 474–480.

Laird, D. A. and Drexel, H. (1934). Experiments with food and sleep. 1. Effects of varying types of food in offsetting sleep disturbance caused by hunger pangs and gastric distress in children and adults. *J. Amer. diet. Ass.*, **10**, 89–99.

Lehmkuhl, R. A. (1935). Comparison of sleep and wakefulness in normal and decerebrated birds. *Fiziol. Zh. S. S. S. R.*, **19**, 622–631.

Leyton, G. B. (1946). Effect of slow starvation. *Lancet*, **2**, 73–79.

Lipscomb, F. M. (1945). Medical aspects of Belsen concentration camp. *Lancet*, **2**, 313–315.

Maliniak, S. (1934). Observations sur la mobilité dans le sommeil. *Archs. Psychol.*, *Geneve.*, **24**, 177–226.

Marquis, D. P. (1941). Learning in the neonate. The modification of behaviour under 3 feeding schedules. *J. exp. Psychol.*, **29**, 263–282.

Moore, T. and Ucko, L. E. (1957). Night waking in early infancy. *Archs. Dis. Child.*, **32**, 333–342.

Moscowitz, M. J. (1959). Running wheel activity in the white rat as a function of combined food-water deprivation. *J. comp. physiol. Psychol.*, **52**, 621–625.

Nielsen, J. M. and Sedgwick, R. P. (1949). Instincts and emotions in an anencephalic monster. *J. nerv. ment. Dis.*, **110**, 387–394.

Oswald, I. (1962). *Sleeping and Waking*, Elsevier Publ. Co., Amsterdam.

Rice, T. B. (1931). Gentle sleep: a third lesson in relaxation in a reformed insomniac. *Hygeia (Chicago)*, **9**, 461–463.

Richter, C. P. (1927). Animal behaviour and internal drives. *Rev. Biol.*, **2**, 307–342.

Russell Davis, D. (1951). *Studies in malnutrition, Wuppertal 1946-49. VIII. Emotional disturbances and behavioural reactions*, M. R. C. Special report series No. 275. H. M. Stationery Office, London, pp. 147–164.

Shirley, M. (1928). Studies in activity. II. Activity rhythms: Age and activity; activity after rest. *J. comp. Psychol.*, **8**, 159–186.

Siegel, P. S. and Steinberg, M. (1949). Activity level as a function of hunger. *J. comp. Psychol.* **42**, 413–416.

Skinner, B. F. (1936). Conditioning and extinction and their relation to drive. *J. gen. Psychol.*, **14**, 296–317.

Southwell, P. R., Evans, C. R. and Hunt, J. N. (1972). Effect of a hot milk drink on movements during sleep. *Brit. med. J.*, **2**, 429–431.

Stanley, L. L. and Tescher, G. L. (1932). What to eat on going to bed. *Calif. west. Med.*, **36**, 318–319.

Treichler, F. R. and Hall, J. F. (1962) The relationship between deprivation, weight loss and several measures of activity. *J. comp. physiol. Psychol.*, **55**, 346–349.

Wada, T. (1922). Experimental study of hunger and its relation to activity. *Arch. physiol.*, **8**, 1–65.

Wald, B. and Jackson, G. (1944). Activity and nutritional deprivation. *Proc. Nat. Acad. Sci., U. S. A.*, **30**, 255–263.

Warner, L. H. (1928). A study of hunger behaviour in the white rat by means of the observation method. *J. comp. Psychol.*, **8**, 273–299.

CHAPTER 6

Some problems in the measurement of sleep, activity, nutrition and mood

Attempts at measurement of sleep, activity, nutrition and mood pose certain major methodological problems. Tools are required which are sufficiently subtle and sensitive to do justice to the complexity of the phenomena under inspection. Such instruments need to be reliable, consistently reproducing the same information when used under identical circumstances, and valid, measuring what they purport to measure. There are, broadly speaking, two ways of seeking such information in respect of all four fields.

The first method is that of *measurement through report* either by the subject, an interviewer or an observer. Clearly such information is liable to subjective distortion on the part of the subject, the observer or both. Although this is a criticism that can readily be levelled so far as areas of sleep, activity and nutrition are concerned, in the area of mood the report of the subject has a special subjective validity.

The second method involves *physical measurement*. It will sometimes be possible to measure the variable directly but otherwise indirect measurement is necessary e.g. the use of weighing scales as a mechanical measure in the direct investigation of population body weight characteristics as compared with their use to measure changes in body weight as a function of metabolic activity; or the estimation of catecholamine levels in the blood as a chemical correlate of stress of which disturbance of mood may be a feature.

Sleep

The simplest methods in the measurement of sleep include questionnaires and analogue scales. The importance has been stressed (Lasagna, 1956) of having clearly defined questions. For example, enquiry about 'time of *final* waking in the morning' often elicits a different response from a question such as 'What time did you wake up?' Reliable questionnaires have now been widely developed in this field but the problem of validity remains.

For instance, it has been reported (Imboden and Lasagna, 1956) that depressed subjects sometimes grossly underestimate the duration of sleep and indeed in this group of patients complaints of insomnia may reach delusional proportions (Lewis, 1931). However, despite the doubt thereby cast upon the validity of such information, clinical judgements are often made on the basis of subjective sleep reports and the effects of treatment thereafter evaluated on the basis of changes in them. For instance, the specific complaint of early morning waking is often taken as one important indication that electroconvulsive therapy is likely to be of help for patients with severe depression, in spite of the fact that continuous all-night EEG recordings will usually show that the sleep disturbance is distributed throughout the night.

Meanwhile some investigators have emphasized the relatively high validity of subjective reports of aspects of sleep. In a study of 18 depressed patients, Hinton (1962) found that the patients made a mean estimate of the duration of their sleep which was only a few minutes shorter than the estimate of nurses observing them. Indeed Hare (1955) found a positive correlation of 0.70 between patients' and nurses' estimation of the duration of sleep and the other findings of Hinton and Marley (1959) also support this. Exton-Smith and coworkers (1953) and Haider (1967) have also found satisfactory correlations between such 'objective' and 'subjective' measures of sleep. However, whilst Costello and Selby (1965) found that in a group of depressed patients there was a positive correlation of 0.69 between patients' and nurses' estimate of time spent awake in bed, the correlation between patients' and nurses' estimate of time of waking was only 0.17.

Grosz and Grossman (1964) stressed the possibility of observer bias influencing data collected. For instance it has been shown (Cox and Marley, 1959; Samuel, 1964) that the observer rates sleep and wakefulness largely on the basis of the movement of the subject, yet it is clear that a patient may lie still yet be wide awake, or alternatively be moving yet remain asleep.

Methods of assessing sleep by measuring the perception of an arousing stimulus have been described (Strauss, Eisenberg and Gennis, 1955; Lindsley, 1957) but these have the obvious disadvantage of possibly waking the patient. The mechanical measurement of sleep has been attempted in several ways. The electroencephalogram aims at recording cerebral electrical changes during sleep. Otherwise, attempts have been made one way and another to detect bodily movement during sleep. The measurement of such movement is not of course a direct measurement of sleep, but motility during sleep has been shown to bear a reciprocal relationship to the depth of sleep as measured electroencephalographically (Loomis, Harvey and Hobart, 1937; Blake, Geard and Kleitman, 1939; Coleman, Gray and Watanabe, 1959; Oswald and coworkers, 1963), although its magnitude and duration is not consistently related to the degree of EEG change in depth of sleep (Hoffman and coworkers, 1956). Such techniques are considered in the next section, which is concerned with the measurement of activity.

The continuous all-night electroencephalogram provides the most direct measurement of duration and depth of sleep and sleep may thus be classified according to the characteristics of the sleep EEG record (see Chapter 1). However, it is a technique that has disadvantages. The need to have electrodes

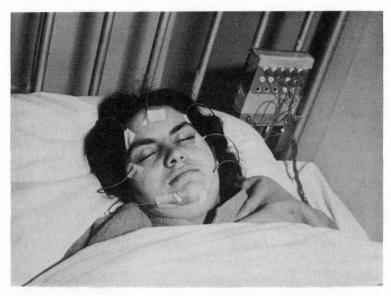

Figure 22. Electrode placements for a sleep EEG; an eighth electrode, not evident in the picture, is attached to a point on the crown of the head. Most subjects adapt remarkably well to being tethered in this way but their sleep . nevertheless usually remains affected by the experimental conditions

attached to the scalp throughout the night produce a 'laboratory' situation which may in itself affect the quality and duration of sleep (Figure 22). A trained technician is required to operate the machine which produces large amounts of data, the interpretation of which is to some extent subjective and the quantification of which is laborious. Oswald and coworkers (1963) undertook a page-by-page analysis of no less than 13 miles of EEG paper in a study involving only six patients.

It may be concluded that there is sometimes only limited agreement between the findings from different methods used in the measurement of sleep. The continuous all-night electroencephalogram, patients' sleep reports and the measurement of nocturnal motility all provide different information about sleep. The EEG provides reliable and valid data on neurophysiological aspects of sleep. Although the patients' sleep report may not tally with this information, it may nevertheless be fundamental as a reflection of his personal experience. Measures of gross nocturnal restlessness and also more subtle bodily movements provide information about aspects of sleep and wakefulness. Maximum information may be obtained by a combination of methods each of which should be treated independently.

Activity

The total organization of musculo-skeletal activity in the individual is complex and attempts at measurement may focus on some specific qualitative or quantitative aspects or else be directed at a more global assessment of such activity. Qualitative abnormalities are common in some neuropsychiatric pathological states and are referred to briefly in Chapter 5. This section is concerned primarily with the quantitative and global assessment of musculo-skeletal activity.

The complexity of bodily activity presents serious problems in its measurement outside the controlled laboratory situation. Such difficulty is also contributed to by the frequent alterations in activity which occur not only from moment to moment but also during the day under the influence of diurnal and possibly also ultradian body rhythms. For example state's of severe depression are often characterized by a reduction of psychomotor activity in the morning which becomes steadily less marked as the day progresses. Such changes during the day are usually less evident than the contrast between activity during wakefulness and sleep. Indeed the assessment of the duration of reduced activity during the sleep period has been used by some as a measure of the duration of sleep. However, the correlation between observed inactivity at night and sleep is clearly not a very high one. Not only may a subject lie still in bed yet be wide awake but he may also display restlessness whilst asleep. In spite of these observations it has been shown (Cox and Marley, 1959; Samuel, 1964) that the observer rates sleep and wakefulness largely on the basis of nocturnal motility. In spite of the difficulties for a subject or an observer in accurately rating activity, once again current clinical practice is largely based on report and observation and such information can be useful. In the light of its possible inaccuracy it is probably best to use a simple scoring system of broad categories. For example it should be possible with reasonable accuracy to categorize a subject on a three-point scale of 'over-activity', 'normal activity' and 'reduced activity', or alternatively use a linear visual analogue scale. It may be possible to obtain reasonable accuracy if a limited enquiry is directed to specific aspects of activity such as the amount of time a subject spends lying down or sitting in a chair during a specific period.

At one stage the authors made an attempt at assessment of more global 24-hour activity levels in a group of psychiatric in-patients. A questionnaire (Table 6) was devised to be completed jointly by the patient, the nursing staff and occupational therapist. A relatively arbitrary loading was given to each item and the scores derived were then combined to provide an activity index score. Although somewhat more sophisticated than the simple rating scale previously described, in common with other questionnaires based on report and observation this approach remains limited by its subjective nature.

Mechanical methods for measuring activity can be used to provide information, often usefully, in conjunction with the more subjective methods. Some such devices are applicable mainly to laboratory conditions. In such instances the impact of the experimental situation and the limitations it imposes on the freedom of movement of the subject, may clearly affect the activity of the subject. Many of these techniques are concerned with the measurement of nocturnal activity whilst the subject is anyway usually confined to one

Table 6. A questionnaire designed to allow rating of activity
of a patient over 24 hours

Name .... Date ....

Time spent in bed at night	
Time spent asleep at night	
Time spent in bed during day	
Time spent asleep during day	
Time spent in O. T.	
Type of activity O. T.	
Time spent ambulent	
Time spent sitting	
Pedometer score	

Brief description of patient's activity during day:

Signature ....

room and is mainly in bed. It has previously been mentioned that measurement of nocturnal motility has been used as an indicator of sleep and Cox and Marley (1959) found that motility scores correlated highly (r = 0.81) with the night nurses' independent estimate of sleep. Although they also found that the patient's own estimate of the soundness of his sleep did not tally with such scores, Samuel (1964) found a positive correlation between motility scores and both nurses' and patients' assessment of sleep.

The technique of measurement of nocturnal motility was pioneered by Szymanski in 1914, who described an apparatus consisting of a chair strung from a beam and the measurements of its pendulum movement. Although earlier methods usually involved entirely mechanical transmission, most reports described the translation of bed spring movement into electrical signals. The apparatus is attached to the springs of the bed and not to the subject, who therefore has complete freedom of movement (see Figure 24). Scores are provided, which can be separated for periods throughout the night, and which reflect bed spring movement. This information is quantitative and a score over unit time gives no information allowing one to distinguish between types of body movement, e.g. a small number of major body movements and a large number of small movements.

A technique which provides this latter kind of information is that of time-lapse cinematography. In the method of Southwell, Evans and Hunt (1972) one frame was taken every 15 seconds and the film then subsequently run back and body movements categorized into big movements and small movements. Apart from the fact that this technique only samples movements and provides no information regarding events between frames, it is limited by the fact that the scoring of movements is subjective. Photographic and similar techniques can clearly be adapted for use during the day, but require that the subject remains within the experimental situation.

Under laboratory conditions the tension and activity of specific muscles may be measured by the technique of electromyography but this provides little information about the activity of the subject as a whole. Another method in which the subject has freedom of activity relies on the measurement of accumulated heart rate over unit time. However, cardiac output and in particular heart rate are dependent upon a number of factors of which only one is musculo-skeletal tonus and activity and so this method also has limitations.

Perhaps the most widely used mechanical device and one which allows the subject complete mobility is the pedometer. This machine works on the pendulum principle and in appearance and size is similar to a stop watch. It is pinned to the outer clothing in the region of the iliac crest and registers hip movement during walking. It can be calibrated to the subject's stride and thus can provide a measure of distance walked. It is limited by the fact that it only records hip movement and incorrect use of the device including its positioning can give rise to spurious scores.

It may be concluded that all the methods described have their limitations. There is as yet no entirely satisfactory way of assessing total activity but, especially when applied in combinations, some of the techniques described can together provide reasonably valid information.

Nutrition

Assessment of the state of obesity of the individual is often basic practice in the nutrition clinic. Despite the multiplicity of its determinants it is a useful quantitative index of the individual's overall nutritional state and changes thereof. Body weight is the index of obesity most commonly measured, and information on this may be acquired by observation, report or mechanical measurement.

Simple observation may allow a fairly accurate judgement to be made as to whether the subject is overweight, of average weight or underweight but, as is the case if the subject is weighed, may not serve to differentiate, for instance, between overweight associated with an excess of adipose tissue, muscle and fluid. Furthermore repeated observations of this kind are unlikely to give accurate information about small changes in weight.

The accuracy with which a subject is able to report his weight depends on a number of factors. If he has recently been weighed on scales, such information is likely to be reasonably accurate, as it may also be if weight has remained more or less constant. The subject who infrequently weighs himself and in whom weight fluctuations are common, may be unable to provide accurate information especially in the area of weight change. The accuracy of such information is also likely to be influenced by the subject's perception of his body shape and his wishes in respect of his weight. It has been shown (Slade and Russell, 1973) for instance, that groups of patients with primary disorders of weight have a distortion of their body image and perceive themselves as fatter than they really are, and that such reports can be significantly affected by the nature of a perceived meal independent of its calorific content (Crisp and Kalucy, 1974).

Accurate information of body weight may be obtained by mechanical measurement using weighing scales. Repeated measurement directed at eliciting weight change should be carried out under standard conditions, to take into account such factors as clothing, meal time, etc. If body weight is used as an index of body shape, then height must be taken into account. Indices of body shape include ponderal index $\left(\dfrac{\text{Height}}{\text{Weight} \times \frac{1}{3}}\right)$ and Quetelet's Index $\left(\dfrac{\text{Weight}}{\text{Height}^2}\right)$, the latter having the theoretical advantage of being correlated highly with body weight and being relatively independent of height (Khosla and Lowe, 1967). If a comparison is to be made between the individual's weight and general population weight characteristics, then age and sex need to be taken into account as well as height, and reference made to tables providing matched population mean weights, e.g. Kemsley (1951). Average weights as distinct from 'ideal' weights (see Chapter 1) probably fluctuate in time under the influence of social, cultural and economic factors and so may be 'out-of-date'.

However, as already indicated, although body weight can be used to provide an index of body shape, it does not necessarily give accurate information about the state of obesity which is a degree of overweight associated with excess adipose tissue. A variety of techniques exist which measure aspects of the degree of adiposity. As the density of body tissues differ, assessment of body density can provide some relative information about the contributions of fat and muscle in the individual. Thus a person's volume can be calculated by total immersion in water and the subsequent measurement of the volume of displaced water. Then, if body weight is known, density can be calculated. Clearly this technique has limited application.

A number of laboratory methods exist for the measurement of total body water. These methods involve the ingestion of a substance and the measurement of its subsequent dilution in the body fluids. From this information, lean body mass may be calculated and subsequently an index of adiposity derived. These techniques are elaborate and require considerable precision and laboratory facilities.

Simpler techniques in the measurement of body fat are those which attempt to measure the thickness of subcutaneous fat in various body sites (Sinclair, 1948; Keys and Brozek, 1953), the assumption being that the site or sites sampled are representative. A radiographic technique may be used but the more practical and popular method (Tanner, 1953) involves the measurement

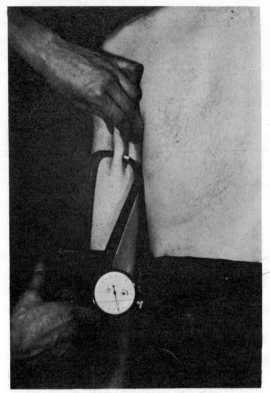

Figure 23. Measurement of skinfold thickness over
the triceps using a caliper

of skinfold thickness using calipers (Figure 23). The correlation between caliper measurement and direct measurement of fat width by X-ray is high (Tanner and Whitehouse, 1962). The most popular sites for measurement include the triceps and subscapular regions. The technique is a relatively reliable one, especially in the lower range of measurement. However, the proposition that the measured skinfold thickness in one or two such specific sites is highly correlated with total amount of adipose tissue is not always correct.

The measurement of body weight, body shape or adiposity provides a general nutritional indicator of the balance of anabolic and catabolic activities in the body. The measurement of food intake provides direct information concerning the intake side of the energy equation. Reports of dietary intake among the general population are probably often inaccurate. This is certainly the case in some psychiatric patients such as those with severe depression or paranoid psychosis in whom perceptive processes may be distorted. Obese subjects often underestimate the amount they consume and conversely patients with anorexia nervosa often exaggerate their dietary intake. Accurate information concerning dietary intake can only be obtained in the controlled laboratory situation and even then it may not be easy to consistently monitor and control the patient. It is even less easy to control fluid intake which, of course, directly affects body weight. Psychogenic polydipsia is a phenomenon which not uncommonly occurs in anorexia nervosa and may be evoked as a mechanism either to assuage overwhelming hunger or to cause the misleading impression that the subject has gained weight as a result of increased calorie intake. Self-induced vomiting or purging behaviour is also common in this population as a means of avoiding weight gain, often despite an apparently adequate food intake. Such behaviour may be difficult to detect as it is often secretive and denied by the patient. Although this is a description of behaviour in a relatively small disturbed population, in the investigation of nutritional intake it is always important to balance food intake against loss in vomit and faeces.

This section has been limited to a discussion of some measures having to do with those aspects of nutritional status which are central to the present monograph.

Mood

Moods are states of feeling usually associated with individual experience and as such they are in some ways unique to that individual. They cannot be measured in absolute terms although their indicants can sometimes be quantified precisely. The measurement of a mood usually includes both qualitative and quantitative features. Measurement may be made by self-rating, by observer rating, or by the measurement of physiological accompaniments of the mood. As mood is a subjective experience, the subject's report of his feelings potentially has a personal validity that cannot be disputed. Difficulty in communication and distortion, wittingly or unwittingly, are factors which can contribute to a discrepancy between self-report and other measurement, raising doubts on the accuracy of the reported feeling. Even if the indicant of the mood is accepted as what the person says he feels and the language of communication is defined, consistency of report or reliability may be difficult to establish as moods are ever fluctuating.

In clinical practice, most attention has been directed to measurement in the areas of feelings of *anxiety* and *depression* as well as more general traits such as *neuroticism* and *extroversion/introversion* which often serve between them to differentiate those with such disordered moods from others. Although these latter dimensions are regarded by some as measures of enduring personality traits, transient changes which reflect alterations in mood do occur. A questionnaire to be completed by the subject and which measures them as specifically named factors is the Eysenck Personality Inventory, the EPI (Eysenck and Eysenck, 1964). This questionnaire also incorporates a *lie* scale, high scores on which may indicate a response in terms of ideal self-concept, rather than candid self-appraisal (Dicken, 1959). The EPI does not distinguish between categories of feelings and is therefore of limited use to the psychiatrist who is concerned with defining diagnostic categories that appear to him to have clinical validity. The Middlesex Hospital Questionnaire (MHQ) (Crown and Crisp, 1966) is a self-administered rating scale designed to try and meet this clinical need. It provides scores on six scales: *anxiety, phobic, obsessional, somatic, depression* and *hysteria.* Two well validated self-rating questionnaires measuring *depression* are the Beck Depression Inventory (Beck and coworkers, 1961) and Zung Depression Scale (Zung, 1965).

In the measurement of *anxiety* Taylor's manifest anxiety scale (Taylor, 1953) has been widely used, and scores have been shown to reflect well-reported physiological accompaniments of anxiety (Buss and coworkers, 1955). Amongst other specific feelings Caine, Foulds and Hope (1967) developed a questionnaire measuring *hostility* and the direction of its expression.

Such moods and indeed the vast range of other moods, can also be measured conveniently by using a linear visual analogue scale (Zealley and Aitken, 1969). Most usually the feeling is rated on a ten centimetre line, the ends of which are defined as representing the extremes of mood under consideration. Ratings made by an observer may be based not only on verbal information provided spontaneously by the patient or in response to questioning, but also on the patient's behaviour and appearance. Information recorded by an observer is, of course, influenced by his bias. Reliability can be ascertained by comparing the ratings of two independent observers. On the whole such schedules take longer to complete than many self-rating scales and may thereby be unsuitable for frequent administration. Other observer rating scales include the Hamilton Rating Scales for *depression* (Hamilton, 1960) and *anxiety* (Hamilton, 1959).

Questionnaires and rating scales are clearly useful in the measurement of mood. Self-rating scales may be limited by the doubtful reliability of the informant. The account he provides of his symptoms may not accord with that given by other informants or the clinician's impressions. He may be defensive and reluctant to reveal his inner experiences or alternatively he may exaggerate or overemphasize his feelings. A further limitation of such questionnaires is rooted in the fact (Cronbach, 1942) that some individuals have a tendency to agree or disagree with propositions put to them, irrespective of their content. It is possible that such a tendency can be reduced by the careful design of the questionnaire. Social desirability is a factor which may influence scores, the subject attempting to depict himself in a favourable light by faking good.

In multiple response scales it has been shown that some subjects show a preference for central positions, whilst others prefer the extreme positions at the end of the scale. These are some of the shortcomings of questionnaire and rating scales. Meanwhile it is often useful to record both self-reported ratings and observer ratings of moods.

Physiological or biochemical changes accompanying changes in mood may be used as indicators of the mood. Psychophysiological techniques include the measurement of forearm blood flow and skin conductance. Forearm blood flow may be measured using a venous occlusion plethysmograph (Kelly, 1967). It has been shown to be a sensitive index of anxiety which is associated with an increase in flow, and has a close association with subjective ratings of anxiety (Gelder and Mathews, 1968). Skin conductance which is dependent on the number of active sweat glands also rises with anxiety, and a close temporal relationship can be shown between a psychogalvanic response (PGR) and an anxiety-provoking stimulus so that the former is often taken as an acceptable alternative unit measurement of such mood.

However, although both these techniques are sensitive to changes in anxiety, they are not specific to this feeling state and reflect more general stress, and in particular measure arousal which may or may not be associated with a subjective feeling of anxiety. For example both skin conductance and forearm blood flow are high in hysterical patients who display a bland or indifferent mood rather than overt anxiety.

Biochemical techniques to measure such end effects as cortisol and nor-adrenalin levels and responsivity may also be used to measure stress and autonomic activity (Levi, 1973). Such measures are not, however, specific indicants of changes in mood.

In conclusion, a combination of techniques may provide most information in the measurement of moods. The choice of techniques will be limited by such factors as the variability of mood. Aitken and Zealley (1970) have said that response to stress is best monitored by both psychophysiological and self-report measures, that anxiety traits are best measured by self-rating and physiological means; whilst depression is best quantified by observer and self-rating scales.

References

Aitken, R. C. B. and Zealley, A. K. (1970). Measurement of moods. *Brit. J. Hosp. Med.*, **4**, 215–224.

Beck, A. T., Ward, C. H., Mendelson, M., Mock, J. and Erbaugh, J. (1961). An inventory for measuring depression. *Arch. gen. Psychiat.*, **4**, 561–571.

Blake, H., Gerard, R. W. and Kleitman, N. (1939). Factors influencing brain potentials during sleep. *J. Neurophysiol.*, **2**, 48–60.

Buss, A. H., Wiener, M., Durkee, N. and Baer, M. (1955). A measurement of anxiety in clinical situations. *J. cons. Psychol.*, **19**, 125–129.

Caine, T. M., Foulds, G. A. and Hope, K. (1967). *Manual of the Hostility and Direction of Hostility Questionnaire (HDHQ)*, University of London Press, London.

Coleman, P. D., Gray, F. E. and Watanabe, K. (1959). EEG amplitude and reaction time during sleep. *J. appl. Physiol.*, **14**, 397–400.

Costello, C. G. and Selby, M. M. (1965). The relationship between sleep patterns and reactive and endogenous depression. *Brit. J. Psychiat.*, **111**, 497–501.

Cox, G. H. and Marley, E. (1959). The estimation of motility during rest or sleep. *J. Neurol. Neurosurg. Psychiat.*, **22**, 57–60.

Cronbach, L. J. (1942). Studies of acquiescence as a factor in the true-false test. *J. educ. Psychol.*, **33**, 401–415.

Crown, S. and Crisp, A. H. (1966). A short clinical diagnostic self-rating scale for psycho-neurotic patients. *Brit. J. Psychiat.*, **112**, 917–923.

Crisp, A. H. and Kalucy, R. S. (1974). Aspects of the perceptual disorder in anorexia nervosa. *Br. J. med. Psychol.*, **47**, 349–361.

Dicken, C. F. (1969). Simulated patterns on the Edwards Personal Preference Schedule. *J. appl. Psychol.*, **43**, 372–378.

Eysenck, H. J. and Eysenck, S. B. J. (1964). *Manual of the Eysenck Personality Inventory*, University of London Press, London.

Exton-Smith, A. N., Hodkinson, H. M., Cromie, B. W. and Curwen, M. P. (1963). Controlled comparisons for four sedative drugs in elderly patients. *Brit. med. J.*, **2**, 1037–1040.

Gelder, M. G. and Mathews, A. M. (1968). Forearm blood flow and phobic anxiety. *Brit. J. Psychiat.*, **114**, 1371–1376.

Grosz, H. J. and Grossman, K. G. (1964). The source of observer variation and bias in clinical judgement. 1. The item of psychiatric history. *J. nerv. ment. Dis.*, **138**, 105–113.

Haider, I. (1967). Safe night sedation for elderly psychiatric patients. *Med. Dig., Lond.*, **13**, 69–71.

Hamilton, M. (1959). The assessment of anxiety states by rating. *Brit. J. med. Psychol.*, **32**, 50–55.

Hamilton, M. (1960). A rating scale for depression. *J. Neurol. Neurosurg. Psychiat.*, **23**, 56–62.

Hare, E. H. (1955). Comparative efficacy of hypnotics; a self-controlled self-recorded clinical trial in neurotic patients. *Brit. J. prev. soc. Med.*, **9**, 140–141.

Hinton, J. M. (1962). Sleep and motility in depressive illness. *Proc. R. Soc. Med.*, **55**, 907–910.

Hinton, J. M. and Marley, E. (1959). The effects of meprodamate and pentobarbitone sodium on sleep and motility during sleep. A controlled drug trial with psychiatric patients. *J. Neurol. Neurosurg. Psychiat.*, **22**, 137–140.

Hoffmann, B. F., Suckling, E. E., Brooks, C. McC., Koenig, E. H., Coleman, K. S. and Treumann, H. J. (1956). Qualtitative evaluation of sleep. *J. appl. Psysiol.*, **8**, 361–368.

Imboden, J. and Lasagna, L. (1956). An evaluation of hypnotic drugs in psychiatric patients. *Bull. Johns Hopkins Hosp.*, **99**, 9.

Kelly, D. H. W. (1966). The technique of forearm plethysmography for assessing anxiety. *J. Psychosom. Res.*, **10**, 373–382.

Kemsley, W. F. F. (1951). Body weight at different ages and heights. *Ann. Eugen.*, **16**, 316–334.

Keys, A. and Brozek, J. (1953). Body fat in adult man. *Physiol. Rev.*, **33**, 245–325.

Khosla, T. and Lowe, F. R. (1967). Indices of obesity derived from body weight and height. *Brit. J. prev. soc. Med.*, **21**, 122–128.

Lasagna, L. (1956). A study of hypnotic drugs in patients with chronic diseases. *J. chron. Dis.*, **3**, 122–133.

Levi, L. (1973). Stress, distress and psychosocial stimuli. *Occup. ment. Hlth.*, **3**, No. 3, 2–10.

Lewis, A. (1931). *A clinical and historical survey of depressive states based on the study of 61 cases*, M. D. Thesis, Univ. Adelaide.

Lindsley, O. R. (1957). Operant behaviour during sleep: a measure of depth of sleep. *Science, N. Y.*, **126**, 1290–1291.

Loomis, A. L., Harvey, E. N. and Hobart, G. A. (1937). Cerebral states during sleep as studied by human brain potentials. *J. exper. Psychol.*, **21**, 127–144.

Oswald, I., Berger, R. J., Jamarillo, R. A., Keddie, K. M. G., Olley, P. G. and Plunkett, G. B. (1963). Melancholia and barbiturates: a controlled EEG, body and eye movement study of sleep. *Brit. J. Psychiat.*, **109**, 66–78.

Samuel, J. G. (1964). Sleep disturbance in depressed patients: objective and subjective measures. *Brit. J. Psychiat.*, **110**, 711–719.

Sinclair, H. M. (1948). Assessment of human nutrition. *Vitamin and Horm.*, **6**, 101.

Slade, P. D. and Russell, G. F. M. (1973). Experimental investigations of bodily perception in anorexia nervosa and obesity. *Psychother. Psychosom.*, **22**, 359–363.

Southwell, P. R., Evans, C. R. and Hunt, J. N. (1972). Effect of a hot milk drink on movements during sleep. *Brit. med. J.*, **2**, 429–431.

Strauss, B., Eisenberg, J. and Gennis, J. (1955). Hypnotic effects of an antihistamine— Methapyrilene hydrochloride. *Ann. intern. Med.*, **42**, 574–582.

Szymanski, J. S. (1914). Eine methode zur undersuchung der ruhe und aktivitaetsperioden bei Tieren. *Pflügers Arch. ges. Physiol.*, **158**, 343–385.

Tanner, J. M. (1953). Growth of the human at the time of adolescence. *Lect. Sci. Basis Med.*, **1**, 308–385.

Tanner, J. M. and Whitehouse, R. H. (1962). Standards for subcutaneous fat in British children. *Brit. med. J.*, **1**, 446–450.

Taylor, J. A. (1953). A personality scale of manifest anxiety. *J. abnorm. soc. Psychol.*, **48**, 285–290.

Zealley, A. K. and Aitken, R. C. B. (1969). Measurement of mood. *Proc. R. Soc. Med.*, **62**, 993–996.

Zung, W. W. K. (1965). A self-rating depression scale. *Arch. gen. Psychiat.*, **12**, 63–70.

CHAPTER 7

Present studies

An initial clinical observation (Crisp, 1967) was made, that sleep disturbance, particularly early morning waking but also interrupted sleep, as well as restlessness during the day, are features of patients suffering from anorexia nervosa, although rarely presented in the form of a complaint. In a study of 60 patients, 80 per cent reported waking up by 6.0 a.m. and nearly 40 per cent reported broken sleep. Insomnia was not clearly related to factors such as age, duration of illness, food patterns or type of diet, and could not be entirely explained as a result of affective disturbance as only ten patients in the series showed evidence of clinical depression.

On the basis of these findings, an hypothesis was erected that a relationship exists between changes in nutritional status and sleep patterns in a general psychiatric population as well as in patients suffering from primary disorders of weight. Although such changes in nutrition and sleep would be more common in some diagnoses, the relationship was hypothesized to span the range of psychiatric diagnosis. Specifically, it was predicted that a relationship exists between total duration of sleep and weight change in the direction of weight loss and reduction in sleep as well as weight gain and increase in sleep, and between time of waking and weight change in the direction of weight loss and early waking as well as weight gain and later waking. Furthermore, it was predicted that this relationship is closer than that between either of these characteristics and any one psychiatric diagnosis of feeling state. In these instances one-tailed tests of statistical significance were to be used. Where other measures of sleep and nutritional status were to be examined, two-tailed tests would be employed.

Two complimentary groups of studies were planned. Firstly intensive studies of small groups of psychiatric in-patients suffering from primary disorders of weight, and secondly studies of a large number of general psychiatric out-patients.

Thus it was planned to investigate further (Study 1) the seeming clinical relationship between nutrition and sleep, which had been identified within the anorexia nervosa population, by detailed and careful study of a small number of anorexia nervosa patients undergoing restoration of weight to a normal level. Furthermore it was decided to similarly investigate a number of massively obese patients undergoing weight loss.

At the same time it was planned to investigate (Study 2) a series of psychiatric out-patients in detail, in respect of their psychiatric status and other aspects of their mental states, and reports of their sleep patterns and body weight, including changes, if any, during the course of their illness. In addition accurate measurements of weight, height and skinfold thickness would be made. It was also planned to examine aspects of this population's nutritional characteristics in relation to current psychiatric status and mood characteristics as well as examining detailed aspects of current sleep and weight in relation to psychiatric state and mood ratings.

References

Crisp, A. H. (1967). The possible significance of some behavioural correlates of weight and carbohydrate intake. *J. Psychosom. Res.*, **11**, 117–131.

CHAPTER 8

Study I: Methodology

Small numbers of patients were studied in depth during their period of in-patient treatment. The treatment programme (with certain specified exceptions—see Chapter 9) for the anorexia nervosa patients has been described in detail elsewhere (Crisp, 1967a, 1970). It involves restoration of weight to matched population mean level in each instance. The patient remains in bed during this time, eating a diet containing normal amounts of carbohydrate. She and her family are involved in psychotherapy. On reaching 'target' weight she is slowly mobilized. The in-patient programme for obesity has also been detailed elsewhere (Crisp, 1967b; Crisp and Stonehill, 1970). It involves the patient remaining ambulant, consuming a 500-calorie diet daily containing a normal proportion of carbohydrate, and being involved in individual psychotherapy and the in-patient unit milieu programme. In all instances the subject's height is measured accurately on admission. Their unclothed weight is measured twice weekly and at other times as necessary on accurate weighing scales.

Investigations involved concurrent study of aspects of the subjects' sleep and sometimes their daytime activity; also aspects of psychoneurotic status, mood, personality and behaviour. The specific measuring instruments and the contexts within which they were used are described below. Where instruments were specifically developed by ourselves they are described in more detail; the others are described briefly and with appropriate reference to other sources.

Sleep

1. Self-report   A sleep questionnaire was devised (Table 6), bearing in mind the requirements for such an instrument outlined in Chapter 6. Subjects completed the questionnaire following a night's sleep, often on a routine twice a week basis, and at other times following each of five consecutive nights spent in the sleep laboratory. Under these latter circumstances and in order to allow for adjustment to these special experimental conditions, the sleep questionnaires on the first two nights of each period of study were discarded.

2. Sleeping encephalogram   Standard sleep EEG records were obtained (see Crisp, Stonehill and Fenton, 1971) within certain of the substudies to be described.

3. *Nocturnal motility* This was measured by a motility bed developed for the purpose and described in detail elsewhere (Crisp, Stonehill and Eversden, 1970). A 28.5 mm (1.125 in.) diameter brass tube is connected by a universal joint to the underside of the centre of the springs of a standard hospital bed (Figure 24). The tube passes through a 38.0 mm (1.50 in.) deep P.T.F.E. collar which is rigidly supported by a steel frame underneath the bed (Figure 25). Light from a festoon bulb passes through evenly spaced slits in the brass tube to pairs of photodiodes embedded in the collar wall (Figure 26). The photodiode pulses are processed electronically and recorded with relatively slow electromagnetic counter printers, or a timer counter with print-out facilities.

Four separate detection channels are provided, each with a different slit and photodiode spacing. The slit spacings chosen were 4, 8, 12 and 16 mm and the corresponding photodiode spacings 2, 4, 6 and 8 mm. Small movements involving individual shifts greater than 2 mm and less than 4 mm in the height of the bed springing are only detected by the most sensitive channel (2 mm diode spacing) while large movements (greater than 16 mm) are detected by all four channels. In order to avoid repetitive counting of small amplitude oscillations in bedspring movement two photodiodes are provided for each channel,

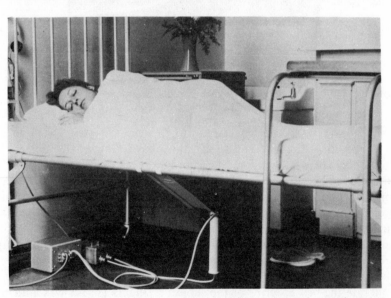

Reproduced by kind permission of the Editor, *Med. & biol. Engng.*

Figure 24. The motility bed.
(From Crisp, A. H., Stonehill, E. and Eversden, I. D. (1970). The design of a motility bed including its calibration for the subject's weight. *Med. and biol. Engng,*, **8**, 455–463.)

70

Figure 25. Bedspring movement detector (From
Crisp, A. H., Stonehill, E. and Eversden, I. D.
(1970). The design of a motility bed including its
calibration for the subject's weight. *Med. and
biol. Engng.*, **8**, 455–463.)

and to record a single event a slit must have sequentially passed both
photodiodes. There is, therefore, no record if the slit oscillates back and forth
over a single photodiode. Furthermore a minimum movement for detection
is imposed upon each channel which is equal to the spacing between the
photodiodes.

Since we were dealing with subjects whose weight was going to change
considerably (e.g. being almost doubled in some instances in the group of
anorexia nervosa patients, and being reduced by about one third so far as some
of the obese patients were concerned), it was considered especially important
to calibrate the bed in terms of the subject's weight. Thus it was anticipated
that, for a given movement on the bed, the amount of motility recorded would be
importantly affected by the subject's weight. At the same time the possibility
that a patient's height might affect the recording of a given movement was also
investigated. In the event height was not found to be a significant factor but
weight was. A satisfactory formula was derived allowing correction of all

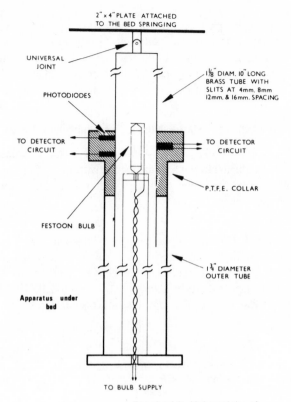

Figure 26. Diagrammatic representation of bedspring movement detector
(From Crisp, A. H., Stonehill, E. and Eversden,
I. D. (1970). The design of a motility bed including
its calibration for the subject's weight. *Med. and
biol. Engng.*, **8**, 445–463.)

motility scores to a standard weight for the bed being used (see again Crisp,
Stonehill and Eversden, 1970). All motility scores referred to in the present
study have been adjusted in this way. The bed was located in a single room
within the sleep laboratory and subjects were studied for periods of five
consecutive nights, again the first two nights' records being discarded.

Daytime Activity

This was measured in certain substudies in either one or two ways:

1. *Questionnaire* As described in Chapter 6 a questionnaire (Table 6)
was devised to be completed jointly by the patient, the nursing staff and the
occupational therapist. Scores were combined to provide an activity index.

2. *Pedometer* The patient wore a pedometer each day from the time of getting up until going to bed. The pedometer score was transcribed numerically every day. The pedometer was not adjusted for the patient's stride and therefore the scores obtained were not measures of actual distance. The recordings however provided information concerning change in activity day by day.

Aspects of Psychoneurotic Status, Mood, Personality and Behaviour

1. *MHQ (Middlesex Hospital Questionnaire)* This was used as a measure of psychoneurotic status. In particular, for the purposes of this study, it provides measures of *anxiety* and *depression* through scales which emphasize mood items (see Chapter 6).

2. *EPI (Eysenck Personality Inventory)* This was used as a measure of more stable personality characteristics, identified as the dimensions of 'neuroticism' and 'extroversion/introversion' respectively (see Chapter 6).

In addition, in one substudy a modification (Russell, 1967) of the Phipps behaviour chart was used to rate aspects of mood and behaviour.

References

Crisp, A. H. (1967a). Anorexia nervosa. *Hosp. med.*, **May**, 713–718.

Crisp, A. H. (1967b). The possible significance of some behavioural correlates of weight and carbohydrate intake. *J. Psychosom. Res.*, **11**, 117–131.

Crisp, A. H. (1970). Anorexia nervosa: 'Feeding disorder', 'Nervous malnutrition' or 'Weight phobia'? *World Review of Nutrition and Dietetics*, **12**, 452–504.

Crisp, A. H. and Stonehill, E. (1970). Treatment of obesity with special reference to seven severely obese patients. *J. Psychosom. Res.*, **14**, 327–345.

Crisp, A. H., Stonehill, E. and Eversden, I. D. (1970). The design of a motility bed including its calibration for the subject's weight. *Med. and Biol. Engng.*, **8**, 455–463.

Crisp, A. H., Stonehill, E. and Fenton, G. W. (1971) The relationship between sleep, nutrition and mood: a study of patients with anorexia nervosa. *Postgrad. med. J.*, **47**, 207–213.

Russell, G. F. M. (1967). The nutritional disorder in anorexia nervosa. *J. Psychosom. Res.*, **11**, 141–149.

CHAPTER 9

Study I: Weight and sleep changes in anorexia nervosa and obesity

Anorexia Nervosa

A. The first investigation reported here concerns ten female anorexia nervosa patients studied before and after a period (8-11 weeks) of treatment involving restoration of their weight to the matched mean population weight for their height and age.

These patients, aged 22 ± 4 years, were treated in a standard manner by bed rest, chlorpromazine, refeeding on a 3,000 calorie 'normal' diet, and regular psychotherapy. All patients achieved their matched population mean weight during treatment and maintained it together with normal eating patterns during the immediate post-treatment period. Before treatment and again immediately after treatment, each patient stayed for 5 successive nights in a single quiet room containing the 'motility bed', nine of the patients received no night sedation and the tenth received the same hypnotic after treatment as before. Chlorpromazine was stopped at least 2 weeks before the second investigation in each case.

Each patient retired to bed between 10.0 p.m. and 10.30 p.m., the 'motility bed' was switched on and the patient left to waken spontaneously in the morning. In the morning the patient was required to complete the questionnaire providing information about the previous night's sleep. During the investigation periods, the patient completed two other questionnaires, namely the Middlesex Hospital Questionnaire (MHQ) and the Eysenck Personality Inventory (EPI).

Results

1. *In relation to patients' self-reports of sleep* Mean values of the various sleep items were calculated for the last 3 nights of each 5-night period before and after treatment for the 10 patients. Table 7 shows the mean pretreatment and post-treatment values for weight, sleep items, MHQ and EPI scores on the 10 patients. The mean group weight increased from 39.9 Kg to 54.4 Kg, a statistically significant change ($p < 0.001$). The group mean total duration of sleep per night increased from just over $6\frac{1}{2}$ hours to just over $7\frac{1}{2}$ hours and this is statistically significant at the 1 per cent level. It is apparent that the mean

Table 7. Mean weight, sleep patterns, psychiatric status and personality and significance of difference in 10 patients with anorexia nervosa before and after treatment (Crisp and Stonehill, 1971)

	Pre-treatment	Post-treatment	Significance (p)
Weight	39.9 kg	54.4 kg	< 0.001
Total sleep	6 hr 32 min	7 hr 35 min	< 0.01
Time to fall asleep	67.7 min	38.5 min	< 0.10
Broken sleep	15.8 min	6.8 min	< 0.10
No. sleep interruptions	1.27	1.06	N.S.
Time of final waking	6.10 a.m.	6.38 a.m.	< 0.10
Total time in bed	8 hr 29 min	8 hr 54 min	N.S.
Total time awake	127.5 min	77.5 min	< 0.02
Anxiety	7.1	5.0	< 0.10
Phobic	2.5	2.7	N.S.
Obessional	9.6	8.0	N.S.
M.H.Q. Somatic	4.6	1.5	0.05
Depression	7.5	5.2	< 0.05
Hysteria	6.1	6.3	N.S.
Total	37.8	28.8	< 0.05
E.P.I. N	12.1	9.6	N.S.
E	6.3	12.1	< 0.001

group total change in sleep reflects changes occurring throughout the night: the pretreatment delay in falling asleep of over one hour falling to just over half an hour in the post-treatment period; the mean pretreatment reported duration of interrupted sleep falling from 16 minutes to 7 minutes post-treatment; similarly final waking in the morning changing from just after 6.0 a.m. pretreatment to after 6.30 a.m. post-treatment. These differences failed to reach statistical significance with the numbers involved (p < 0.10). On the MHQ all scales except the phobic and hysteria scales revealed a decrease in mean score in the post-treatment period but only the somatic and depression scores reached significance (p < 0.05). None of the patients were, however, judged to be suffering from severe depression on clinical grounds during the pretreatment period. Furthermore, when the mean pretreatment MHQ scores of this group of patients are compared with the mean MHQ scores of 24 psychoneurotic in-patients who were not diagnosed as suffering from depressive illness (Table 8), there is no difference in the depression scores between the two groups. In other respects the patients scored significantly lower than psychoneurotic subjects. On the EPI there was a mean increase in the E score after treatment which is significant at the 0.1 per cent level.

During treatment all patients achieved their matched population mean weight but the weight increase necessary for this varied between patients. Table 9 is a chart displaying the changes between pretreatment and post-treatment weights, sleep patterns, MHQ and EPI scores in the ten patients.

Table 8. Mean MHQ scores, standard deviations and significance of differences between 10 in-patients with anorexia nervosa before treatment and 24 non-depressed psychoneurotic in-patients (Crisp and Stonehill, 1971)

	A	P	O	S	D	H
10 Inpatients with anorexia nervosa before treatment aged 22 ± 4 yr	7.5 ± 3.5	2.5 ± 1.9	9.6 ± 3.1	4.6 ± 3.1	7.5 ± 2.7	6.1 ± 2.7
24 non-depressed psychoneurotic inpatients aged 30 ± 9 yr	12.5 ± 1.8	9.0 ± 4.0	9.3 ± 3.0	9.3 ± 4.2	8.2 ± 2.7	7.5 ± 3.3
Probability (P)	< 0.001	< 0.001	N.S.	< 0.001	N.S.	N.S.

A = anxiety; P = phobic; O = obessional; S = somatic; D = depression; H = hysteria.

When the amount of weight increase is correlated with each of the changes in sleep patterns (Table 10), the main and significant correlation (with the small numbers involved) is between amount of weight increase and later time of waking up in the morning ($r = 0.89$; $p < 0.001$). Changes in weight, total sleep, time to fall asleep, interrupted sleep and time of final waking failed to correlate at a significant level with any of the MHQ and EPI score changes. When the correlation between increase in weight and later time of waking up in the morning is calculated with the effect of the MHQ depression scores partialled out, it remains significant at the 0.1 per cent level ($r = 0.88$).

2. *In relation to motility scores* Mean values of the motility scores for the whole stay on the bed, the first and second halves of the stay, and each hour of the stay, were calculated for the last three nights of each 5-night period before and after treatment for the ten patients. Overall nocturnal motility (Figure 27) is approximately halved after treatment ($p < 0.05$). Figure 28 shows that this reduction is greatest in the first half of the night ($p < 0.01$) although still significant ($p < 0.05$) in the second half. More detailed analysis (Figure 29) shows that this reduction holds hour by hour and is greatest in hours 1 and 2.

Table 11 displays the changes in weight and motility scores for the ten patients. Changes in nocturnal motility, even during the first half of the night, do not show such a close relationship to change in weight as is the case with patients' self-reports of sleep. In particular it can be seen (Table 9) that patient No. 1, who reported sleeping much longer (over two hours) after treatment, at the same time showed a striking increase in nocturnal motility (Table 11). Changes in motility scores did not correlate significantly with any of the changes in MHQ or EPI scores.

3. *Relationship between patient self-reports of sleep and nocturnal motility* Results tended to be in support of a reciprocal relationship between patients'

Table 9. Changes in weight, sleep patterns, psychoneurotic status and personality in 10 patients with anorexia nervosa before and after treatment (Crisp and Stonehill, 1971)

No.	Wt. (Kg)	Total sleep (min)	Time to fall asleep (min)	Broken sleep (min)	No. of sleep interruptions	Time of waking (min)	M.H.Q.							E.P.I.	
							A	P	O	S	D	H	Total	N	E
1	+20.9	+140	−75	0	+1.7	+87	−5	+1	+1	−9(−7)	−7(−5)	+4	−15	−10	+6
2	+14.5	+123	−100	+4	+0.3	+20	−6	+1	0	−3(−1)	0(0)	0	−8	−3	+3
3	+14.5	+11	+10	−2	−2.3	+22	−3	−3	−5	−9(−8)	−1(−1)	−3	−24	−1	+11
4	+6.3	−40	+6	0	−0.3	−28	+1	−1	+2	+2(+2)	−1(−1)	0	+3	+5	+6
5	+20.9	+70	+1	−4	−1.0	+68	+4	0	+4	−1(−1)	+1(+1)	+2	+6	0	+2
6	+17.2	+46	+4	−38	+0.3	+12	−6	0	−6	−3(−3)	−4(−2)	+2	−17	−6	+4
7	+13.1	+18	−3	−3	−0.3	+7	0	0	−2	0(0)	0(0)	0	−2	+1	+3
8	+7.3	+80	−87	−15	−0.7	−20	−1	+3	+3	−4(−4)	0(0)	−2	−1	−3	+7
9	+17.2	+133	−30	−27	+1.0	+76	−3	0	−5	−1(−1)	−6(−4)	+3	−11	−1	+6
10	+14.5	+48	−18	−5	−0.7	+23	−4	0	−8	−3(−3)	−5(−3)	0	−20	−7	+10

( ) = Score with sleep questions removed.

Table 10. Coefficients of correlation and significances between increase in weight and aspects of improved sleep in 10 patients with anorexia nervosa during treatment (Crisp and Stonehill, 1971)

Sleep item	r	p
Total sleep	0.56	< 0.1
Time to fall asleep	0.06	N.S.
Broken sleep (min)	0.16	N.S.
No. sleep interruptions	0.33	N.S.
Time of waking	0.89	< 0.001

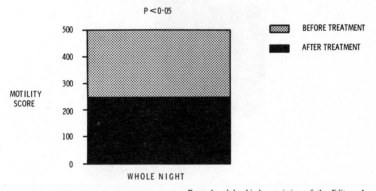

Reproduced by kind permission of the Editor, *J psychosom. Res.*

Figure 27. Mean total nocturnal motility score over 3 consecutive nights, standardized for weight, in 10 patients with anorexia nervosa before treatment and after restoration of bodyweight (Crisp and Stonehill, 1971)

reports of duration of sleep and nocturnal motility scores. However, correlations between such reports and motility scores were low and did not reach statistical significance. For example, the correlation between decrease in nocturnal motility scores after treatment and increase in self-reported sleeping time in the ten patients was + 0.29 only. A similar low correlation was obtained between changes in motility scores during the first half of the night and changes in reported times taken to fall asleep, as well as changes in motility scores during the second half of the night and reported changes in times of waking. Furthermore, when pretreatment motility scores were compared with pretreatment sleep self-reports, correlation coefficients obtained were again not significant. Similar findings were obtained when post-treatment motility scores and self-reports were compared.

B. The second investigation reported here describes work done collaboratively with Dr. George W. Fenton, Senior Lecturer at the Institute of Psychiatry, London (Crisp, Stonehill and Fenton, 1971), and concerns EEG

78

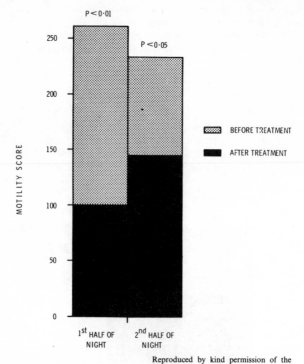

Figure 28. Mean nocturnal motility score for the first
and second halves of the night over 3 consecutive nights,
standardized for weight, in 10 patients with anorexia
nervosa before treatment and after restoration of body-
weight (Crisp and Stonehill, 1971)

studies on five patients (four females and one male) admitted to a psychiatric
metabolic unit for treatment* of primary anorexia nervosa. Their ages were
14, 16, 17 (male), 18 and 36 years. Each was seen 10-14 days after admission.
At bedtime chlorided silver 'stick-on' electrodes were applied to the scalp in
the right frontal, central, parietal and occipital areas as well as the superior
and lateral aspects of both orbits. These were connected to an eight-channel
Offner type T electroencephalograph in an adjacent room.

The patient then retired to bed and bipolar recordings were performed
continuously throughout the night, for at least seven hours or longer until
the patient woke spontaneously. This procedure was repeated during the
following three nights, recordings being carried out on each patient during
four consecutive nights. When the patients had gained weight, but not
necessarily a weight amounting to their matched population weight, and prior

---

* We are greatly indebted to these patients and to Professor G.F.M. Russell for permission to
study them in this way whilst under his care.

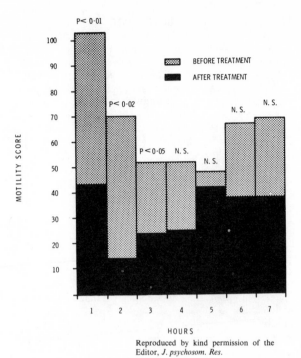

Figure 29. Mean hourly nocturnal motility score over 3 consecutive nights, standardized for weight, in 10 patients with anorexia nervosa before treatment and after restoration of body-weight. Mean hourly pretreatment scores throughout night significantly greater than hourly post-treatment scores (p < 0.01)(Crisp and Stonehill, 1971)

to discharge from hospital, this procedure was repeated, each patient having a further four consecutive all-night sleep recordings performed. The interval between the two series of tests varied from 6 weeks to 3 months. Treatment consisted of refeeding with a high protein and high carbohydrate diet. No daytime psychotropic drugs were prescribed. One patient received a hypnotic, the dose being maintained unchanged throughout the study. Four of the patients responded well to this regime, gaining at least 10 kg. One failed to show any appreciable weight gain. Daily ratings of mood and behaviour were carried out using a modification of the Phipps behaviour chart (Russell, 1967) and each patient's mood was also assessed independently by a psychiatrist unaware of the EEG findings, during an interview conducted on the day of the first of each series of recordings.

All sleep records were examined by a single investigator, who rated the depth of sleep for each 20-second period throughout the night using the Loomis, Harvey and Hobart (1937) classification. Data obtained from the first night

80

Table 11. Changes in weight and nocturnal motility scores in 10 patients with anorexia nervosa following treatment (Crisp and Stonehill, 1971)

No	Wt (Kg)	Total nocturnal motility	Motility 1st half night	Motility 2nd half night
1	+20.9	+267	+ 27	+203
2	+14.5	−267	−183	− 84
3	+14.5	− 55	− 50	− 5
4	+ 6.3	−123	− 73	− 50
5	+20.9	−462	−141	−322
6	+17.2	−259	−130	−127
7	+13.1	−765	−387	−378
8	+ 7.3	−599	−480	−118
9	+17.2	− 52	− 12	− 40
10	+14.5	−207	−191	− 16
Correlation coefficient between increase in weight and decrease in motility		+0.35	+0.52	+0.09

Table 12. Time in each stage of sleep in minutes. Mean values for twelve nights in four subjects with anorexia nervosa (Crisp, Stonehill and Fenton, 1971)

Stage	Before treatment	After treatment	Significance (p)
Awake	28.5	5.9	< 0.01
A	27.9	3.1	< 0.005
B	88.8	93.4	NS
C	170.9	156.4	NS
D	65.2	89.1	< 0.05
E	33.5	73.4	< 0.005
REM	63.1	78.1	< 0.05

of each four-night series were discarded in order to allow for the so-called 'first night effect', ratings from subsequent nights being used.

Results

Results obtained from the four patients who gained weight were examined separately, the fifth patient who gained no weight being treated as a control subject. In the light of the initial observation and the results of the sleep self-report study, these large amounts of EEG data were treated so as to provide

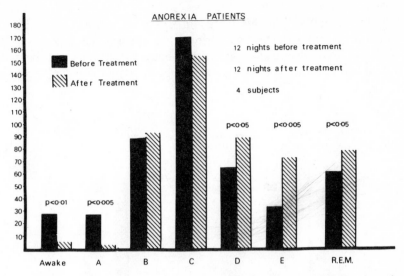

ANOREXIA PATIENTS

Before Treatment

After Treatment

12 nights before treatment

12 nights after treatment

4 subjects

Reproduced by kind permission of the Editor, *Postgrad. med. J.*

Figure 30. Mean duration in minutes of each stage of sleep in anorexia nervosa patients (4 subjects) 12 nights before treatment and 12 nights after treatment. (Crisp, Stonehill and Fenton, 1971)

twelve separate items of information both before and after treatment on the four patients, the corresponding nights of investigation before and after treatment being compared on each occasion.

The total time asleep per night, defined as the duration of time spent in stages B (light sleep), C (medium sleep), D (deep sleep), E (very deep sleep) and REM (rapid eye movement sleep) was increased following treatment, the mean for the initial twelve nights being 6.3 hr compared with the post-treatment value of 7.0 hr. This difference is significant at the 5 per cent level.

Figure 30 displays in histogram form the amount of time spent in the various stages of sleep throughout the night, and Table 12 shows this data in tabular form with probability levels concerning the significance of the differences. Before treatment significantly more time was spent awake ($p < 0.01$) and in stage A (drowsy) ($p < 0.005$), whilst on retest an increase in duration of time spent in stages D ($p < 0.05$) and E ($p < 0.005$) was apparent. The amount of REM sleep was also greater after refeeding ($p < 0.05$). The latency of onset of both slow wave and REM sleep was altered following weight gain. The mean length of time from the onset of the recording to the first 60 seconds of C stage sleep was significantly reduced from 27.4 minutes before treatment to 7.6 minutes after treatment ($p < 0.025$). The mean latency of onset of REM appeared to be delayed pretreatment and occurred after 147.5 minutes, but was reduced to 77.6 minutes post-treatment ($p < 0.02$). The mean number of shifts of stage of sleep per hour was also reduced from 43.1 before treatment to 36.1 after treatment but this trend did not reach statistical significance. The amount of time spent awake during the night was greatest during the first and last hours, especially the latter (Figure 31). Before treatment the mean total amount of time spent awake during the seventh hour of recording

Pattern of wakefulness throughout the night.

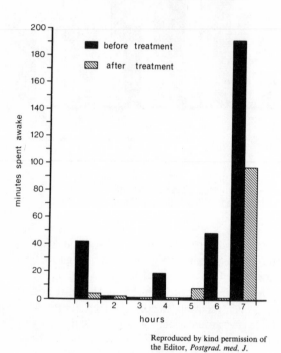

Reproduced by kind permission of
the Editor, *Postgrad. med. J.*

Figure 31. Pattern of wakefulness throughout the night: the total number of minutes spent awake during each hour in 12 nights of all-night recordings in 4 patients with anorexia nervosa. (Crisp, Stonehill and Fenton, 1971)

was 16.0 minutes and this was reduced to 8.2 minutes after treatment, but this trend did not reach statistical significance.

The patient whose weight remained essentially unchanged can be regarded as a control subject and Figure 32 reveals that there was no major change in the sleep pattern.

Ratings of the patients' mood states carried out by the nursing staff and

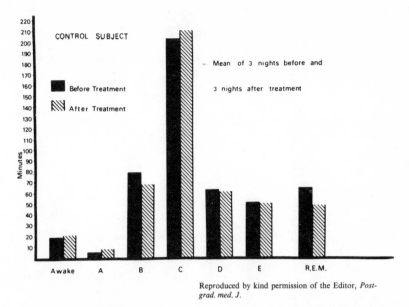

Figure 32. Control subject: mean of 3 nights before and 3 nights after treatment. (Crisp, Stonehill and Fenton, 1971)

assessment of the mental state carried out by the psychiatrist before and after treatment revealed no consistent mood changes.

Obesity

A. In this investigation three patients with massive obesity were treated on an in-patient basis and in the way described in Chapter 8. They were each studied in detail over a number of months as they lost weight. Patients completed the sleep questionnaire twice weekly, providing information about the previous night's sleep. Daytime activity was measured by the pedometer and by the activity rating scale previously described (see Chapter 8, page 72). Menstrual activity was recorded and personality, psychoneurotic and mood status were assessed at intervals, using the MHQ and the EPI (and in one instance the MPI, an earlier version of the EPI).

Results

Case No. 1. Results of the measurements on this patient are displayed in Figure 33.

She was in hospital on a 500-calorie diet for a total of 6 months and lost weight steadily from over 110 Kgs down to 73.14 Kgs. The average total nightly sleep per fortnight is charted. This shows an initial reported reduction in sleep, then a brief period of increased sleep followed by a steady decrease

84

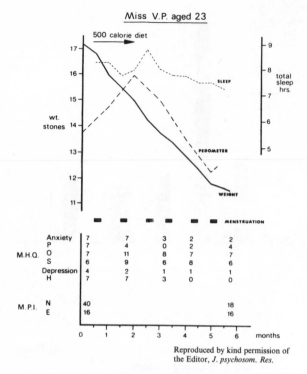

Figure 33. Chart of changing weight, daytime activity, menstrual activity, sleep, psychoneurotic state and personality during a period of 6 months in-patient treatment in Case No. 1. (Miss V. P.) (Crisp and Stonehill, 1970)

in total sleep from the third month onwards until her discharge from hospital. At no time during treatment did the patient take night sedation. On admission her average duration of nightly sleep was over 8 hours and this decreased to just over 7 hours by the time of discharge from hospital. The decrease in duration of sleep is not accompained by a high depression (D) score at any time but instead with progressive lowering of anxiety scores (A) and (P) from neurotic to normal levels and an associated lowering of the depression score.

Daytime activity as measured by the pedometer showed an increase initially followed by a steady fall from the end of the second month onwards, this being from a point in time about two weeks prior to the onset of the progressive reduction in reported duration of sleep.

Menstrual activity remained regular.

Case No. 2. During the course of 4 months hospitalization this patient lost weight from over 92 Kgs to just over 73 Kgs (Figure 34). There was a transitory increase in weight when the diet was increased from 500 calories to 1000 calories during the last 3 weeks.

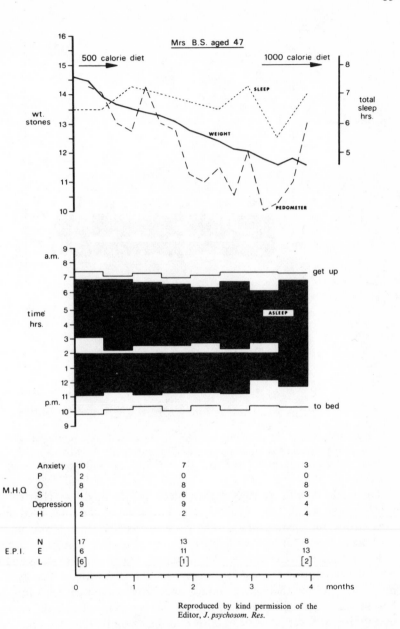

Reproduced by kind permission of the
Editor, *J. psychosom. Res.*

Figure 34. Chart of changing weight, daytime activity,
sleep, psychoneurotic state and personality during a
period of 4 months' in-patient treatment in Case No. 3
(Mrs. B. S.) (Crisp and Stonehill, 1970)

86

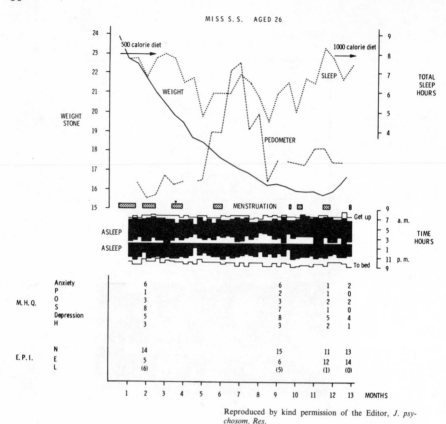

Figure 35. Chart of changing weight, daytime activity, menstrual activity, sleep, psychoneurotic state and personality during a period of 12 months' in-patient treatment in Case No. 2 (Miss S. S.) (Crisp and Stonehill, 1970)

Total duration of average nightly sleep per fortnight as charted showed no consistent trend. Total broken sleep is depicted by the condensed unshaded area within the shaded block. The patient was frequently given nitrazepam 5-10 mg at night during the course of her third month in hospital in response to her complaint of inability to sleep soundly. The increase in sleep and lack of broken sleep during the last two weeks is associated with an increased calorie intake. In addition there is a trend towards progressively earlier waking during hospitalization until the last two weeks. This is consistent with the information that in the early period of hospitalization the patient had to be wakened in the morning whereas later on she was waking spontaneously earlier. Anxiety (A) and depression (D) scores on the MHQ fell steadily during treatment from neurotic to normal levels.

There was an overall decrease in daytime activity measured by the pedometer during treatment, until the calorie intake was increased, at which point the pedometer score correspondingly rose. This is consistent with the patient's report of increasing weakness occasionally associated with hypotensive episodes on the 500 calorie diet, and an increase in well-being when the calorie intake was increased. There appears to be some parallel course between increase of daytime activity and increase of sleep, and decrease of daytime activity and decrease of sleep.

No menstrual activity was reported and the patient regarded herself as being in an early menopausal state.

Case No. 3. This patient was in hospital for one year. During this time her weight fell steadily from 152.64 Kgs to under 110 Kgs during the first 8 months. At this point she became unable to remain consistently on the 500-calorie diet and further weight loss was slow. During the last 6 weeks in hospital her weight increased by nearly 6 Kgs. Her total sleep appeared to vary in relation to her nutritional state. There was a decrease in total sleep associated with initial steady weight loss. With an increase in calorie intake and weight during the latter period of her stay and especially during the last 6 weeks, the duration of her sleep increased (Figure 35). The sleep pattern indicates broken sleep, including broken sleep in the early hours of the morning, but charted as in the last case, together with initial insomnia, to be the main feature of the sleep disturbance. From the seventh month onwards the patient was sometimes prescribed nitrazepam 5-10 mg at night in response to her complaint of increasing inability to sleep. Following the patient's initial phase of evident depression, she never again appeared clinically consistently or deeply depressed during treatment although there was a rise in the MHQ depression (D) score, which subsequently fell. This was contributed to by the sleep disturbance as a question on sleep is incorporated in the depression scale.

Daytime activity as measured by the pedometer increased until the seventh month and then declined. These changes were paralleled by the changes in the 24-hour ward assessment of activity charts. During the middle phase of treatment, this patient became more active by day and night.

On admission the patient suffered from menorrhagia. During treatment her periods became shorter and less heavy and she then developed 3-months amenorrhea during the same middle phase of treatment before her periods returned in association with an increased calorie intake. At the same time she complained of dryness and thinness of hair, which was falling out.

B. This study involved the further examination of five obese subjects treated as above and investigated in respect of changes in body weight, nocturnal motility, sleep self-reports (on a twice weekly basis as before) and psycho-neurotic status (MHQ). Nocturnal motility was measured in the way described in Chapter 8. Each of four patients slept, for 5 consecutive nights at approximately monthly intervals, on the motility bed in a single room next to the sleep laboratory. Motility scores (always corrected for body weight) on the first two nights of each 5-night period were discarded and the records of the first 7 hours on the last three nights were examined and average motility scores per night calculated.

88

Results

Sleep reports, Motility, Weight and Mood From inspection of the data obtained there appeared to be a wide range of response between patients in sleep reports and motility recordings during weight loss, although there were no major changes in MHQ scores in any patient during this time. The duration of in-patient treatment varied between 4 months and 8 months, and we therefore decided to examine the average changes in sleep, motility, weight and mood of the patients during the first 4 months when they were all in hospital.

Figure 36 displays the average changes in weight and self-reported total duration of sleep in the five patients. Weight dropped fairly steadily from an average of 100 to 87 Kg after 4 months. Average self-reported total duration of sleep also showed a month by month reduction from 7 hr 20 min in the first month to 6 hr 15 min in the fourth month.

Figure 37 displays the average of three nights' nocturnal motility scores, standardized for weight, at monthly intervals over 4 months in four patients, for whom this information was available, compared with average self-reported duration of interrupted sleep in these patients over the same course of time.

The patterns of motility and broken sleep appear to follow one another closely. Scores are high initially but fall in month 2 and from then on there is a progressive increase both in motility scores and duration of broken sleep.

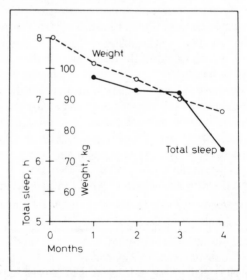

Figure 36. Mean change in body weight and self-reported total duration of sleep per night in 5 obese subjects during 4 months' in-patient treatment for obesity (Crisp, Stonehill, Fenton and Fenwick, 1973)

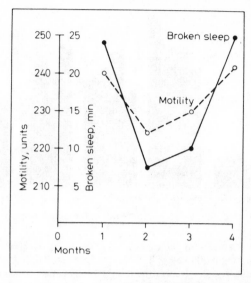

Reproduced by kind permission of
the Editor, *Psychother. Psychosom.*

Figure 37. Mean changes in self-reported duration of broken sleep and recorded nocturnal motility per night in 4 obese subjects during 4 months' in-patient treatment for obesity (Crisp, Stonehill, Fenton and Fenwick, 1973)

The average MHQ scores fluctuated very little during the period of investigation, and therefore were not related to changes in weight or sleep. A correlational matrix was computed between monthly changes in weight, weight change per week, percentage change in excess (in relation to matched population mean) weight, total self-reported sleep, nocturnal motility and MHQ scores in the four patients. This failed to reveal any statistically significant relationships between weight, sleep, motility and MHQ scores.

C. During 8 months' treatment in hospital, one other female patient, aged 26 years and 152 cm in height lost weight from 109 to 76 Kg. EEG recordings were performed for 7 hr after retiring to bed on two consecutive nights at four intervals during the period of hospital treatment. These EEG investigations were conducted together with colleagues from the Institute of Psychiatry (Crisp, Stonehill, Fenton and Fenwick, 1973). On these occasions nocturnal motility was also measured and the patient completed the sleep questionnaire and MHQ. The total sleep time (TST) defined as the duration of time spent in stages 1 (light sleep), 2 (medium sleep), 3 (deep sleep), 4 (very deep sleep) and REM (rapid eye movement sleep) was not significantly different during the series of recordings apart from the initial night during which the subject was becoming acclimatized to the experimental procedure and the lowest TST was recorded. The mean value for all eight nights was 6 hr 25 min.

90

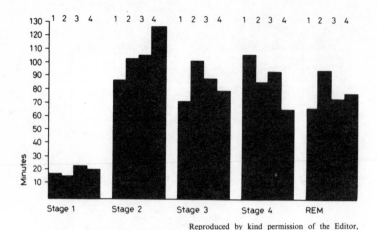

Figure 38. Changes in the pattern of sleep during weight reduction.
1 = April, weight 108.86 kg; 2 = May, weight 100.69 kg; 3 = October,
weight 78.46 kg; 4 = December, weight 76.2 kg. One column = mean
of 2 nights' sleep (Crisp, Stonehill, Fenton and Fenwick, 1973)

The range was 5 hr 31 min to 6 hr 38 min. The duration of reported sleep was
greater than these values on each occasion. There was no consistent change in
the amount of sleep as measured by the EEG during weight reduction. On
most nights more than 85 per cent of recording time was spent asleep. Figure 38
displays the pattern of change within each of the eight nights' sleep and reveals
a number of trends during the course of treatment.

The amount of stage 1 sleep remains essentially unchanged during the series
of recordings. The patterns of stage 2 and stage 4 sleep show changes. There is an
increase of stage 2 sleep associated in time with a relative reduction in amount
of stage 4 sleep. Thus, there is a shift towards lighter slow-wave sleep. This is
consistent with this patient's nocturnal motility recordings. After an initial
high score at the beginning of treatment, followed by a drop in month 2, there
is a steady increase in motility score throughout the treatment period. The
duration of REM sleep shows a transient increase after one month of weight
reduction and then returns to almost the initial levels, and a similar change in
stage 3 sleep is observed. Throughout the course of treatment MHQ scores
remained essentially unchanged.

References

Crisp, A. H. and Stonehill, E. (1970). Sleep patterns, daytime activity, weight changes and
psychiatric status: A study of three obese patients. *J. psychosom. Res.*, **14**, 353–358.
Crisp, A. H. and Stonehill, E. (1971). Aspects of the relationship between psychiatric
status, sleep, nocturnal motility and nutrition. *J. psychosom. Res.*, **15**, 501–509.
Crisp, A. H., Stonehill, E. and Fenton, G. W. (1971). The relationship between sleep,
nutrition and mood: A study of patients with anorexia nervosa. *Postgrad. med. J.*, **47**,
207–213.

Crisp, A. H., Stonehill, E., Fenton, G. W. and Fenwick, P. B. C. (1973). Sleep patterns in obese patients during weight reduction. *Psychother. Psychosom.*, **22**, 159–165.

Loomis, A. L., Harvey, E. N. and Hobart, G. A. (1937). Cerebral states during sleep as studied by human brain potentials. *J. exper. Psychol.*, **21**, 127–144.

Russell, G. F. M. (1967). The nutritional disorder in anorexia nervosa. *J. psychosom. Res.*, **11**, 141–149.

CHAPTER 10

Study II: Aims and methodology

Development of Tools of Enquiry

Questionnaires to be completed by the patient (Patient Questionnaire) and on the basis of interviews (Interviewer Questionnaire) and a Consultant Questionnaire were designed to seek information about the present illness, in the weeks preceding attendance at the out-patient clinic, and at the time of attendance. It was recognized that the validity of such an enquiry is limited by its retrospective and largely subjective nature, and an attempt was made to incorporate some objective measures in the study. The tools of enquiry were carefully developed and tested and the study designed in a way which sought to challenge the patient on areas of information possibly doubtful because of their subjective nature.

Patient Questionnaire

A preliminary questionnaire to be completed by patients, seeking information about sleep, weight and mood states, was developed and administered to 20 psychiatric in-patients. Each patient was interviewed following completion of the questionnaire and questioned about each of the answers he had given with the intention of encouraging him to shift his response. This was undertaken as an attempt to test the viability of the questionnaire as well as the stability and to some extent the validity of each response. This study led to several modifications of the questionnaire and its administration and only questions which appeared unambiguous and showed stability of response on challenge were retained. These questions concerned duration of illness, premorbid and present weight, time of going to bed, time of going to sleep, time of waking up and getting up, and self-ratings of a variety of feeling states on a 4-point scale before the present illness and in recent weeks (Tables 13 and 14).

The questionnaire was presented to the patient in a standard way by first reading a short introduction and explanation sheet with him and then going through the whole questionnaire, item by item, to ascertain that he understood and was able to complete all the questions. The repeat reliability of the questions was investigated by the administration of the questionnaire to 30 new referrals

Table 13. Section 1 of Patient Questionnaire

SECTION 1   NO. 305

HOW LONG DO YOU CONSIDER YOU HAVE HAD YOUR <u>PRESENT</u> ILLNESS ? ... *May 1967 ($\frac{22}{12}$)*

WHAT WAS YOUR WEIGHT <u>JUST BEFORE</u> YOUR PRESENT ILLNESS ?   *14 st. 5 lbs*

WHAT IS YOUR WEIGHT NOW ? *12 st. 2½ lbs.*

	IN THE TIME JUST BEFORE YOUR PRESENT ILLNESS	IN THE LAST FEW WEEKS
WHAT TIME DID YOU USUALLY GO TO BED ?	*11 p.m.*	*11 p.m.*
WHAT TIME DID YOU USUALLY GO TO SLEEP ?	*11.15 p.m.*	*11.15 p.m.*
WHAT TIME DID YOU USUALLY WAKE UP IN THE MORNING ?	*6.00 a.m.*	*5.30 a.m.*
WHAT TIME DID YOU USUALLY GET UP ?	*6.30 a.m.*	*7.00 a.m.*

SECTION 1 OF PATIENT QUESTIONNAIRE

to psychiatric out-patient clinics before the diagnostic interview and again about an hour later after this interview had been completed. The patients were encouraged to make any changes they wished on the second occasion. The average amount of change on all items was fairly small, varying between 0.17 lb. to 0.47 lb. for the weight questions and 1.5 min. and 11 min. for sleep questions. There was no significant difference between the means for

Table 14. Section 2 of Patient Questionnaire

NO. 305

PLEASE RATE YOUR FEELINGS ON THE FOLLOWING SCALE BY PLACING A CROSS (X) IN THE APPROPRIATE COLUMNS CONCERNING:

1. THE TIME <u>JUST BEFORE</u> YOUR PRESENT ILLNESS STARTED
2. THE LAST FEW WEEKS

PLEASE ANSWER <u>EVERY</u> QUESTION.   YOUR FEELINGS RATED SHOULD BE YOUR <u>USUAL</u> FEELINGS DURING THE TIME STATED

	1 IN THE TIME JUST BEFORE YOUR PRESENT ILLNESS STARTED				2 IN THE LAST FEW WEEKS			
	NOT AT ALL	SLIGHTLY	QUITE A BIT	VERY	NOT AT ALL	SLIGHTLY	QUITE A BIT	VERY
FEELING NERVOUS		X						X
FEELING ANGRY	X				X			
FEELING ON TOP OF THE WORLD			X		X			
FEELING EXCITED	X				X			
FEELING SAD	X						X	
FEELING TENSE	X							X
FEELING FIDGETY AND RESTLESS	X					X		
FEELING IRRITABLE	X				X			

SECTION 2 OF PATIENT QUESTIONNAIRE

any item except 'feeling nervous in the last few weeks' following the two administrations of the questionnaire. Product-moment correlations for each item between the first and second administrations were very high, ranging from 0.96 to 1.00 for all items in section 1, but were lower in section 2, ranging from 0.61 to 0.94. It is recognized that the statistical interpretation of this study is of limited value as the high correlations are likely in part to reflect memory. Nevertheless the study confirmed that a variety of patients varying in intelligence and degree of emotional disturbance were able to understand and complete the questionnaire satisfactorily. In spite of the opportunity to change responses after the impact of the diagnostic interview, the overall shift in responses was small, providing some evidence of stability of response and suggesting that it was unnecessary to further modify the questionnaire.

Interviewer Questionnaire

Two questionnaires were developed, one primarily concerned with sleep, and the other with weight, but each also carrying other questions and providing the opportunity for recording additional information. Questions found not to have been readily understood in the Patient Questionnaire were instead included here, together with questions retained in the former questionnaire, since the aim was partly to explore the impact of an interview challenging the validity of this information. The sleep questionnaire also incorporated questions concerning the consumption at night of hypnotics and snacks (Table 15).

Table 15. Interviewer Questionnaire on Sleep

DURATION OF PRESENT ILLNESS _May 1967 (22/12)_   NO. _305_

	IN THE TIME JUST BEFORE YOUR PRESENT ILLNESS STARTED				IN THE LAST FEW WEEKS			
WHAT TIME DID YOU USUALLY GO TO BED ?	11·00 p.m.				11·00 p.m.			
WHAT TIME DID YOU USUALLY GO TO SLEEP ?	11·15 p.m.				11·05 p.m.			
WHAT TIME DID YOU USUALLY WAKE UP IN THE MORNING ?	6·00 a.m.				5·45 a.m.			
WHAT TIME DID YOU USUALLY GET UP ?	6·30 a.m.				7·00 a.m.			
FOR HOW LONG EACH NIGHT WAS YOUR SLEEP USUALLY BROKEN (mins.) ?	5 mins.				15 mins.			
HOW MANY TIMES WAS YOUR SLEEP USUALLY BROKEN EACH NIGHT ?	1				3			
WHAT TIME DID YOU USUALLY HAVE TO GET UP FOR YOUR JOB ETC. ?	7·15 a.m.				7·15 a.m.			
	NEVER	OCCAS-IONALLY	FRE-QUENTLY	ALWAYS	NEVER	OCCAS-IONALLY	FRE-QUENTLY	ALWAYS
DID YOU NEED TO BE WAKENED ?	X				X			
DID YOU DOZE BETWEEN WAKING UP AND GETTING UP ?		X				X		
DID YOU TAKE ANYTHING TO HELP YOU SLEEP ?			X				X	
IF SO, WHAT DID YOU TAKE ? (INCLUDES BOTH SLEEPING PILLS AND DRINK OR SNACK? SPECIFY WHICH AND TIME WHEN TAKEN, INCLUDING REPEATS DURING NIGHT)	Biscuits & cups of tea, approx: ½ hr. before retiring.				Biscuits & cocoa, →			
COMMENT : ___	No sleeping pills				No sleeping pills.			

INTERVIEWER QUESTIONNAIRE ON SLEEP

The weight questionnaire contained questions concerning the subject's weight at varying times and whether or not these estimates were of dressed or undressed weights, as well as questions about psychotropic drug intake and the existence of pain or disease other than the present psychiatric illness. The patient's age, sex and measurement of his height, weight, triceps and subscapular skinfold thickness, and his matched population mean weight (Kemsley, 1951/52), were also recorded on this 2-page questionnaire (Tables 16 and 17).

Table 16. Interviewer Questionnaire on Weight, Page 1

INTERVIEWER QUESTIONNAIRE ON WEIGHT.   PAGE 1.   NO.   *305*

DURATION OF PRESENT ILLNESS *May 1967 ($\frac{22}{12}$)*

WHAT WAS YOUR WEIGHT IN THE TIME JUST BEFORE YOUR PRESENT ILLNESS STARTED ? *13 stones*

IS THIS AN ESTIMATE OF YOUR WEIGHT WITH YOU DRESSED OR UNDRESSED ? *Dressed.*

WHAT IS YOUR PRESENT WEIGHT ? *12 st. 3 lbs.*

IS THIS AN ESTIMATE OF YOUR WEIGHT WITH YOU DRESSED OR UNDRESSED ? *Undressed*

WHAT HAS BEEN YOUR GREATEST WEIGHT EVER EXCLUDE PREGNANCY ? *14 st. 10 lbs.*

HOW OLD WERE YOU AT THIS TIME ? *46.*

WHAT HAS BEEN YOUR LOWEST WEIGHT EVER ? *11 st 12 lbs.*

HOW OLD WERE YOU AT THIS TIME ? *47.*

BY HOW MUCH HAS YOUR WEIGHT CHANGED IN THE LAST FEW WEEKS ? *No change.*

HOW LONG IS "THE LAST FEW WEEKS" ? —

HAS THIS BEEN WEIGHT GAIN WEIGHT LOSS OR BOTH ? —

HOW OFTEN DO YOU WEIGH YOURSELF ? *Once a week.*

WHAT IS YOUR USUAL WEIGHT ? *12 st 5 lbs*

WHAT DRUGS WERE YOU TAKING ?	IN THE TIME JUST BEFORE YOUR PRESENT ILLNESS STARTED	IN THE LAST FEW WEEKS
	Nil	
TRANQUILLISER		*LIBRIUM, 1 cap. t.d.s.*
SEDATIVE		
STIMULANT		
ANTIDEPRESSANT		
ALCOHOL	*Rarely.*	*Rarely.*
HEROIN COCAINE ETC		
UNKNOWN DRUG FOR "NERVES"		
DID THE DRUG MAKE YOU SLEEPY ?	—	*No*

If necessary the questions were clarified or rephrased by the interviewer in discussion with the patient until it was clear that the patient fully understood what specific information was being sought. The patient was told that some of the questions were the same as those he had already answered in the Patient Questionnaire and he now had the opportunity of changing his mind—and he was encouraged to do this.

Both interviewers received practice and training in the administration of the questionnaires. An inter-rater reliability study was not carried out as this was considered unnecessary, for although attempts were made to encourage patients to change their response, the study was not primarily concerned with the differential skills of the interviewers in accomplishing this.

Consultant Questionnaire

A questionnaire on which various aspects of the patient's mental state could be recorded was designed for completion by the consultant following the diagnostic interview. It is current psychiatric convention to place a patient

Table 17. Interviewer Questionnaire on Weight, Page 2

INTERVIEWER QUESTIONNAIRE ON WEIGHT   PAGE 2.   NO. 305

ARE YOU SUFFERING FROM ANY OTHER ILLNESS ? ......Nil......

IF SO SPECIFY. INCLUDING TREATMENT -

MEASURED HEIGHT .5. ft. .9. in.   TRANSFORMATION VALUE (INCHES) ...69.

AGE .48.

SEX ..Male

MEASURED WEIGHT .12. st. .2. lb.   TRANSFORMATION VALUE (POUNDS)...170

TRICEPS SKINFOLD   9.5 mm.   TRANSFORMATION VALUE ...189.:....
      THICKNESS

SUBSCAPULAR SKINFOLD 19.6 mm.   TRANSFORMATION VALUE ..225.:....
         THICKNESS

MATCHED POPULATION MEAN
         WEIGHT 155. lb.

COMMENT :   Seemed definite about weights .

in one or sometimes several diagnostic categories. It was considered that advantage was to be gained by rating every patient on each of a number of commonly used diagnostic categories, thus providing a diagnostic profile of the patient, in addition to ratings on various items of mood and behaviour.

The first part of the questionnaire comprised 19 common diagnostic categories in random order. Space was left for the consultant to insert up to three additional diagnoses. Each patient was to be rated on a 4-point scale for each of the diagnostic categories. The consultant would also be required to make an overall diagnosis (Table 18).

Table 18. Psychiatrist Questionnaire, Part 1

PSYCHIATRIST QUESTIONNAIRE. PART 1. NO. 305

	NOT AT ALL	SLIGHTLY	QUITE A BIT	VERY
CONVERSION HYSTERIA	✓			
ANXIETY STATE		✓		
OBESITY	✓			
HYPOCHONDRIASIS	✓			
ENDOGENOUS DEPRESSION			✓	
MANIA	✓			
CHRONIC SCHIZOPHRENIA	✓			
ANXIETY PHOBIC STATE	✓			
ANOREXIA NERVOSA	✓			
ALCOHOLISM	✓			
ADDICTION (OTHER)	✓			
PSYCHOPATHY	✓			
SEXUAL DEVIATION	✓			
PERSONALITY DISORDER (OTHER)		✓		
OBSESSIONAL STATE		✓		
DEMENTIA	✓			
NEUROTIC DEPRESSIVE REACTION		✓		
PARANOID STATE	✓			
ACUTE SCHIZOPHRENIA	✓			

WHAT IS YOUR OVERALL DIAGNOSIS ? Depression, Obsessional & Anxiety features.

RATER'S NAME STOREY

Table 19. Psychiatrist Questionnaire, Part 2

NO. 305

PSYCHIATRIST QUESTIONNAIRE.   PART 2.

	NOT AT ALL	SLIGHTLY	QUITE A BIT	VERY
TENSENESS			✓	
FLATNESS (AFFECT)	✓			
AGITATION	✓			
ANXIETY			✓	
SADNESS			✓	
ELATION	✓			
WEIGHT LOSS		✓		
ANGER	✓			
EXCITEMENT	✓			
EARLY MORNING WAKING	✓			
DENIAL	✓			
	ABSENT	DIMINISHED	UNCHANGED	INCREASED
SEXUAL ACTIVITY		✓		

RATER'S NAME   STOREY

The second part of the questionnaire consisted of 12 items to be rated on a 4-point scale. These included aspects of the patient's feeling state as in the Patient Questionnaire, but sometimes rephrased, and also ratings of weight loss, early morning waking, denial and sexual activity (Table 19).

The questionnaire was explained to and discussed with the four consultant psychiatrists who agreed to complete it in the main study. They were encouraged to gain experience with it and a reliability study was carried out. In this each psychiatrist was invited to complete the questionnaire on five new out-patients following the diagnostic interview. He then completed a fresh questionnaire a week later, having not seen the patient in the intervening period, but having scrutinized his clinical notes. Inconsistencies in ratings were discussed with each psychiatrist who then rated a further five patients in the same way on two occasions. An error score, the sum of the difference between rating scores on each item on the two occasions, was calculated on each of the 40 patients. A comparison between the error scores on the first 20 patients (five patients per psychiatrist) and the second 20 patients, revealed a fall in total error score from 94 on the first occasion to 63 on the second occasion. This indicated a significant increase in consistency obtained by the four consultants after practice. Rank order correlations for each rating on the two separate occasions revealed a very high level of consistency of ratings on retest. Although this is likely in part to be a function of memory, the study was intended partly to familiarize the consultants with the questionnaire and if necessary enable them to alter their diagnostic interview techniques to seek all the information required. The hope that, by having inconsistencies pointed out, the consultants would become more watchful and consistent was borne out, and it was considered that as a training procedure this was a worthwhile endeavour.

Physical Measurements

Skinfold thickness

Skinfold thickness measurements by calliper, which have been shown to correlate highly with direct measurement of fat width by X-ray (Tanner and Whitehouse, 1962), were made to give an estimate of body fat. The thickness measured depends upon the characteristics of the calliper and in order to obtain maximum consistency between duplicate readings, the Harpenden skinfold calliper (Tanner, 1953) was used. Measurements were made to the nearest 0.1 mm at two sites following the technique described by Tanner and Whitehouse (1962).

(a) Triceps—halfway down the left arm between the tip of the acronium and the top of the radius, with the fold picked up in a line passing directly up the arm from the tip of the olecranon process, with the arm hanging relaxed by the side.

(b) Subscapular—just below the angle of the left scapular, with the shoulder and arm relaxed, the fold being picked up in a vertical line or slightly inclined in the natural cleavage of the skin.

A layer of skin and subcutaneous tissue was pulled away from the underlying muscle by the finger and thumb of the measurer. The thumb and forefinger of the measurer's left hand was placed on the subject's skin just far enough apart so that a full fold was pinched up clear away from the underlying tissue. The fold was pinched up firmly and held between the fingers all the time the measurement was being taken. The callipers were applied to the fold a little below the fingers so that the pressure on the fold at the point measured was exerted by the calliper faces and not the fingers. The right hand fingers were then released from the handle of the calliper to permit the full force of the spring to be exerted on the fold and the dial was then read to the nearest 0.1 mm. The readings were converted to a logarithmic scale as the distribution in the general population is skew, with a long tail of high readings, and duplicate measurements at the same site by the same observer agree more closely for small than for large measurements. The transformation converts the distribution to an approximate standard one (Edwards and coworkers, 1955).

All skinfold thickness measurements were made by E. S. following completion of both Interviewer Questionnaires, and recorded on the Interviewer Questionnaire on Weight in mm. and later transformed to the logarithmic scale.

A reliability study was carried out by E. S. using the Harpenden skinfold calliper. The subjects were 26 adult medical in-patients with a wide age range. Triceps and subscapular skinfold thickness measurements were made during one morning, and the site of measurement was marked with ink. The measurements were then repeated blind 24 hours later. There was no significant difference between the mean measurements in either site on the two occasions, and the coefficient of correlation between duplicate readings was 0.99. The distributions of differences between duplicate readings for measurements grouped in 5 mm ranges, showed an increase in the range and mean difference in proportion to skinfold thickness. This study showed the calliper to be a sensitive instrument which proved reliable in the hands of this experimenter, especially over the lower ranges of skinfold thickness. In comparison with others (Edwards and coworkers, 1955) the present experimenter tended to be less reliable than one observer who had more experience with the instrument, but obtained more consistent measurements than those obtained by different observers.

Measurement of Stature

The patients were measured in their stockinged feet with their heels together, eyes directed forward at their own level, and with instructions to stand erect without making an effort to stretch up. The instrument was a vertical pole fixed to the wall with a horizontal smoothly sliding bar. The pole was graduated in feet, inches and eighths of inches. The investigator's right hand located the vertex of the head while his left hand moved the horizontal bar down to rest there. An attempt was made to exert a reasonable and similar pressure in each case taking into account differences in hair thickness. The measurement was recorded in inches and feet, to the nearest inch, on the Interviewer Questionnaire on Weight.

Measurement of Body Weight

The patients were weighed with coats, jackets and shoes removed on accurate weighing scales. The instrument was a platform weighing scale graduated in stones, pounds and ounces. With the patient standing unsupported on the platform the poises were moved along the weighing beam by the investigator until balance was obtained. The measurement was recorded in stones and pounds, to the nearest pound on the Interviewer Questionnaire on Weight.

Measurement of Body Shape

Quetelet's index, $\dfrac{\text{Weight (lb)}}{\text{Height}^2 \text{ (in.)}} \times 100$, based on measured body weight and height, was used as an index of body shape (Khosla and Lowe, 1967).

Design of Study

The study was carried out in the Psychiatric Out-patient Department of a London teaching hospital. The population investigated consisted of new referrals to the clinics of four consultant psychiatrists. Consecutive referrals were included in the study as far as possible, but patients aged 17 years or less at the time of reported onset of the present illness were excluded to eliminate body growth as a factor influencing weight change. Similarly, patients who reported being pregnant at either of the two periods of time under investigation were eliminated. In addition those patients who reported sleeping predominantly during the day were excluded, although other shift workers who worked less frequently at night were included and were asked to report on night time sleep.

After the patient had booked in at the clinic, the two interviewers introduced themselves to the patient. The patient was told that he would be seen by the consultant psychiatrist later on and that the interviewers were interested in the sleep of patients and in the meantime would like the patient to fill up a questionnaire. The Patient Questionnaire was then introduced by reading the instruction page with the patient, and after going through the questionnaire the patient was left alone in the office to complete it, with instructions to let the interviewers know when he had finished. It usually took about 10 minutes for the patient to complete the first questionnaire. The two Interviewer Questionnaires were then administered consecutively. Both the order in which the questionnaires were given and the order of their allocation to the two interviewers were changed in a random way. Thus each interviewer enquired only about sleep or about weight in any one patient. The investigation was designed in this way in an attempt to control for any bias that either interviewer might have influencing the data collected. Each interview usually lasted between 10 and 15 minutes. After the second interview had been completed, the interviewer scrutinized the Patient Questionnaire and returned it to the patient for completion if there were any omissions or ambiguities. Measurements of height, weight, triceps skinfold thickness and subscapular skinfold thickness were then all made and recorded. The patient was then seen for the diagnostic interview by the consultant psychiatrist. Following this interview, which usually lasted between 45 and 90 minutes, the psychiatrist completed the last questionnaire providing a diagnostic profile together with other details of the patient's mental state.

102

Analysis of Data

All data obtained were transferred to punched cards for computer analysis. Distribution tables together with means and standard deviations of the items investigated were obtained on the first 100 patients and later on the total population. An intercorrelational matrix between the items was prepared on the total population. Based on this matrix, a principal components analysis was carried out. Finally 2×2 contingency tables were prepared on various subpopulations. The Chi square test of statistical significance, corrected for continuity, was applied when numbers were large enough (Siegel, 1956). When numbers were smaller the Fisher Exact Probability Test was utilized. In cases where firm predictions concerning the outcome were made, one-tail tests were utilized; in all other cases two-tailed tests were used.

References

Edwards, D. A. W., Hammond, W. H., Healy, M. J. R., Tanner, J. M. and Whitehouse, R. H. (1955). Design and accuracy of callipers for measuring subcutaneous tissue thickness. *Br. J. Nutr.*, **9**, 133–143.

Kemsley, W. F. F. (1951). Body weight at different ages and heights. *Ann. Engen.* **16**, 316–334.

Khosla, T. and Lowe, C. R. (1967). Indices of obesity derived from body weight and height. *Br. J. prev. soc. Med.*, **21**, 122–128.

Siegel, S. (1956). *Non-parametric statistics for the behavioural sciences*, McGraw-Hill Co. Ltd., Tokyo, p. 110.

Tanner, J. M. (1953). Growth of the human at the time of adolescence. *Lect. Sci. Basis Med.*, **1**, 308–363.

Tanner, J. M. and Whitehouse, R. H. (1962). Standards for subcutaneous fat in British children. *Br. med. J.*, **1**, 446–450.

CHAPTER 11

Study II: Distribution of data

In all, 375 patients (172 men and 203 women) with a mean age of 34 ± 12 years, were investigated. Fifty-nine patients with a mean age of 36 ± 13 years were excluded on a variety of grounds, such as their poor grasp of English or because they had physical diseases affecting their weight.

Distributions and, where appropriate, means and standard deviations were initially calculated in the first 100 patients, and inspection of these data determined aspects of the further plainning of the study, including the definition of initial insomnia as falling asleep at 1.00 a.m. or later and early morning waking as waking at 6.30 a.m. or before, so as to include about a quarter of the population in each definition.

The following data refer to the total population of 375 patients. Tables 20–24 show the distributions of weight and sleep in the first part of the Patient Questionnaire. The mean patient report of weight before the illness was 143 ± 26 lbs. (men 157 ± 22 lbs; women 131 ± 22 lbs), and for the time of attendance was 142 ± 27 lbs. (men 157 ± 23 lbs; women 130 ± 24 lbs). This difference is not statistically significant (Table 20). The distribution of patients' report of weight change since the start of the illness is displayed in Table 25. Sixty-five patients reported having lost 10 lbs. or more and 56 patients having gained 10 lbs. or more since the start of the illness. Although the mean time of going to bed before the illness and in the last few weeks were similar (11.16 p.m. and 11.14 p.m.), 42 patients reported going to bed before 10.00 p.m. and 44 patients after 1.00 a.m. in the last few weeks compared with 18 and 25 patients respectively before the illness (Table 21). The mean time of falling asleep was significantly earlier before the illness (11.53 p.m. $\pm$ 67 minutes) than in the last few weeks (12.13 a.m. $\pm$ 96 minutes) ($p < 0.005$). Although 16 patients reported falling asleep before 10.00 p.m. in the last few weeks compared with six patients before the illness, 61 patients reported falling asleep after 2.00 a.m. in the last few weeks compared with 23 patients before the illness (Table 22). The mean self-reported times of waking just before the illness and in the last few weeks were 7.15 a.m. $\pm$ 75 minutes and 7.14 a.m. $\pm$ 92 minutes and this difference is not significant. Table 23 shows that in the last few weeks 13 patients reported waking before 5.00 a.m. and 46 patients after 9.00 a.m. compared with five and 28 patients respectively in the time before the

Table 20. Distribution of weight before the illness and in the last few weeks (Patient Questionnaire). Total population

Weight (lb)		<98	98–112	112–126	126–140	140–154	154–168	168–182	182–196	196–210	210+
Before Illness	Male	0	0	7	29	42	42	26	16	6	4
	Female	3	30	51	54	30	19	12	1	1	2
	Total	3	30	58	83	72	61	38	17	7	6
Last few weeks	Male	0	1	8	22	48	42	23	15	9	4
	Female	8	35	49	52	26	14	12	2	3	2
	Total	8	36	57	74	74	56	35	17	12	6

Table 21. Distribution of time of going to bed before the illness and in the last few weeks (Patient Questionnaire). Total population

Time	< 9 p.m.	9–10	10–11	11–12	12–1	1–2	2 + a.m.
Before illness	1	17	81	184	67	19	6
Last few weeks	9	33	88	129	72	28	16

Table 22. Distribution of time of going to sleep before the illness and in the last few weeks (Patient Questionnaire). Total population

Time	9 p.m.	9–10	10–11	11–12	12–1	1–2	2–3	3 + a.m.
Before illness	0	6	50	137	120	39	14	9
Last few weeks	5	11	47	98	83	70	39	22

Table 23. Distribution of time of waking up before the illness and in the last few weeks (Patient Questionnaire). Total population

Time (a.m.)	< 3	3–4	4–5	5–6	6–7	7–8	8–9	9–10	10 +
Before illness	3	1	1	21	87	166	68	15	13
Last few weeks	2	1	10	38	92	117	69	25	21

Table 24. Distribution of time of getting up before the illness and in the last few weeks (Patient Questionnaire). Total population

Time (a.m.)	< 5	5–6	6–7	7–8	8–9	9–10	10 +
Before illness	0	9	58	161	103	22	22
Last few weeks	2	5	42	134	92	59	41

Table 25. Distribution of weight change since the start of the illness (Patient Questionnaire).
Total population

	Weight Loss (lb.)					Weight Gain (lb.)			
	40 +	40–30	30–20	20–10	10–10	10–20	20–30	30–40	40 +
Male	0	1	5	17	128	9	10	0	2
Female	2	0	9	31	126	26	6	1	2
Total	2	1	14	48	254	35	16	1	4

illness. Patients reported getting up significantly earlier before the illness, 7.44 a.m. $\pm$ 71 minutes, than in the last few weeks, 8.08 a.m. $\pm$89 minutes ($p < 0.001$). Table 24 shows that 100 patients reported getting up after 9.00 a.m. in the last few weeks compared with 44 patients in the time before the illness. This may partly reflect the fact that some patients had stopped work during their illness and therefore did not need to get up as early.

The distribution of patients' ratings of feelings is displayed in Table 26 and reveals a shift towards feeling more nervous, angry, sad, tense, fidgety and restless and irritable, but less on top of the world and excited in the last few weeks compared with before the illness. It is noteworthy that between a third and a half of the patients reported feeling 'quite a bit' or 'very' nervous, sad, tense, restless or irritable in the time before the illness.

The distribution of items based on the Interviewer Questionnaire on Sleep are displayed in Tables 27–38. The mean reported times of going to bed just before the illness and in the last few weeks were 11.19 p.m. $\pm$ 61 minutes and 11.16 p.m. $\pm$ 81 minutes respectively and this difference is not significant. Forty-seven patients reported going to bed before 10.00 p.m. and 49 after 1.00 a.m. in the last few weeks compared with 19 and 18 patients respectively in the time before the illness (Table 27). The mean reported time of going to sleep was significantly earlier, 11.50 p.m. $\pm$ 66 minutes in the time before the illness, than in the last few weeks when it was 12.07 a.m. $\pm$ 92 minutes ($p < 0.005$). Although 20 patients reported falling asleep before 10.00 p.m. in the last few weeks compared with four patients before the illness, 51 patients reported falling asleep after 2.00 a.m. in the last few weeks compared with 18 patients before the illness (Table 28). The mean reported times of waking up just before the illness and in the last few weeks based on the Interviewer Questionnaire were 7.16 a.m. $\pm$ 67 minutes and 7.19 a.m. $\pm$ 89 minutes respectively and this difference is not significant. Table 29 shows that in the last few weeks eight patients reported waking before 5.00 a.m. and 47 patients after 9.00 a.m. compared with one and 27 patients respectively in the time before the illness. The mean time of getting up was reported by the Interviewer as being significantly earlier before the illness, 7.40 a.m. $\pm$ 69 minutes, than during the last few weeks when it was 8.09 a.m. $\pm$ 88 minutes ($p < 0.001$). Table 30 shows that 97 patients reported getting up after 9.00 a.m. in the last few weeks com-

Table 26. Section 2 of Questionnaire. Distributions on total population (Stonehill, Crisp and Koval, 1976)

Feeling	Before illness				Last few weeks			
	Not at all	Slightly	Quite a bit	Very	Not at all	Slightly	Quite a bit	Very
Nervous	78	169	82	46	26	67	130	152
Angry	167	137	55	16	104	113	93	64
On top of the world	120	119	102	32	245	82	36	11
Excited	125	113	109	27	187	96	59	33
Sad	124	134	71	45	43	95	111	126
Tense	69	128	96	80	16	49	115	194
Fidgety and restless	94	136	86	59	48	63	126	136
Irritable	97	148	85	44	47	90	118	120

Reproduced by kind permission of Editor. *Br. J. med. Psychol.*

Table 27. Distribution of time of going to bed before the illness and in the last few weeks (Interviewer Questionnaire). Total population

Time	< 9 p.m.	9–10	10–11	11–12	12–1	1–2	2 + a.m.
Before illness	2	17	87	163	78	23	5
Last few weeks	11	36	85	125	69	37	12

Table 28. Distribution of time of going to sleep before the illness and in the last few weeks (Interviewer Questionnaire). Total population

Time	<9 p.m.	9–10	10–11	11–12	12–1	1–2	2–3	3 + a.m.
Before illness	1	3	62	143	108	40	12	6
Last few weeks	6	14	46	106	96	56	36	15

Table 29. Distribution of time of waking up before the illness and in the last few weeks (Interviewer Questionnaire). Total population

Time (a.m.)	< 3	3–4	4–5	5–6	6–7	7–8	8–9	9–10	10 +
Before illness	0	1	0	22	98	165	62	14	13
Last few weeks	3	2	3	30	94	133	63	24	23

Table 30. Distribution of time of getting up before the illness and in the last few weeks (Interviewer Questionnaire). Total population

Time (a.m.)	< 5	5–6	6–7	7–8	8–9	9–10	10 +
Before illness	0	11	62	167	92	21	22
Last few weeks	1	3	45	141	88	56	41

Table 31 Distribution of report of duration of interrupted sleep before the illness and in the last few weeks. Total population

Time (min)	0–15	15–30	30–45	45–60	60–90	90–120	120–180	180 +
Before illness	306	20	16	5	13	3	6	6
Last few weeks	262	26	27	13	19	10	15	3

Table 32. Distribution of number of sleep interruptions before the illness and in the last few weeks. Total population

Number	0	1	2	3	4	5	6	7 +
Before illness	278	49	24	19	3	2	0	0
Last few weeks	217	63	43	36	11	1	1	3

Table 33. Distribution of length of time in bed before the illness and in the last few weeks (Interviewer Questionnaire). Total population

Time (hr.)	< 6	6–7	7–8	8–9	9–10	10–11	11–12	12 +
Before illness	4	25	100	142	69	23	11	1
Last few weeks	6	23	81	102	79	34	28	22

Table 34. Distribution of interviewer report of length of time asleep before the illness and in the last few weeks. Total population

Time (hr.)	< 4	4–5	5–6	6–7	7–8	8–9	9–10	10–11	11 +
Before illness	8	8	36	78	130	86	23	5	1
Last few weeks	22	25	36	107	102	42	23	13	5

Table 35. Distribution of need to be awakened before the illness and in the last few weeks (Interviewer Questionnaire). Total population

	Never	Occasionally	Frequently	Always
Before illness	108	74	69	133
Last few weeks	167	54	48	106

Table 36. Distribution of dozing between waking up and getting up before the illness and in the last few weeks (Interviewer Questionnaire). Total population

	Never	Occasionally	Frequently	Always
Before illness	133	123	56	63
Last few weeks	130	101	63	81

Table 37. Distribution of consumption of drink or snack before the illness and in the last few weeks (Interviewer Questionnaire). Total population

	No drink or snack	Bedtime	During night	Bedtime and repeat
Before illness	116	249	2	8
Last few weeks	127	235	2	11

Table 38. Distribution of the consumption of sleeping pills before the illness and in the last few weeks (Interviewer Questionnaire). Total population

	No sleeping pills	Bedtime	During night	Bedtime and repeat
Before illness	346	27	0	2
Last few weeks	284	88	0	3

pared with 43 patients in the time before the illness. The mean reported duration of interrupted sleep was significantly less, 8.9 ± 21 minutes, in the time before the illness than in the last few weeks when it was 19.6 ± 41 minutes (p < 0.001). Twenty-eight patients reported interrupted sleep of 90 minutes or more in the last few weeks compared with 15 patients before the illness (Table 31). Similarly the mean number of sleep interruptions were significantly less, 0.5 ± 0.9 before the illness, than in the last few weeks when it was 0.9 ± 1.3 (p < 0.001). Sixteen patients reported four or more interruptions per night in the last few weeks compared with five patients in the time before the illness (Table 32). Table 33 shows that less patients reported the need to be awakened in the last few weeks compared with before the illness. The increase in spontaneous waking in the last few weeks may be a reflection of the later time reported for getting up. A few more patients reported dozing between waking and getting up in the last few weeks than before the illness but this was not striking (Table 34). There was little difference in the number of patients reporting consumption of drinks or snacks between the two periods of time, about two-thirds of the population reporting that they frequently or always had a drink or snack within two hours of going to bed (Table 35). Eighty-eight patients reported taking hypnotics in the last few weeks compared with 27 patients before the illness (Table 36).

In no instance did the mean sleep item based on the Interviewer report differ significantly from the corresponding item based on the Patient Questionnaire. The mean duration of time spent in bed, from the Interviewer Questionnaire, before the illness was 8 hours 21 minutes and in the last few weeks it was 8 hours 53 minutes. Twenty-two patients reported spending more than 12 hours in bed per night in the last few weeks compared with one patient before the illness (Table 37). The mean duration of sleep in the time before the illness was 7 hours 16 minutes and this is significantly longer than during the last few weeks when it was 6 hours 52 minutes (p < 0.005). However, although 47 patients reported sleeping for less than 5 hours in the last few weeks compared with 16 patients before the illness, 18 patients reported sleeping for more than 10 hours in the last few weeks compared with only six before the illness (Table 38).

The distribution of items on the Interviewer Questionnaire on Weight are displayed in Tables 39–47. The mean report of weight just before the illness was 145 ± 26 lbs. (men 159 ± 22 lbs; women 132 ± 23 lbs), and for the time of attendance was 144 ± 27 lbs. (men 159 ± 23 lbs; women 131 ± 23 lbs). This difference is not significant. These measures correspond closely to the Patient Questionnaire data. These Interviewer weights include clothing, an addition of 4 lbs. being made to any weight reported as undressed. Table 48 shows that 65 patients were reported as having lost 10 lbs. or more and 49 patients as having gained 10 lbs. or more since the illness. The distribution of reported weight change in the last few weeks is displayed in Table 42 and shows that 85 patients reported weight loss, 64 weight gain and 214 no change in weight in the last few weeks. One hundred and seventy patients reported that they weighed themselves monthly or more frequently, including 20 who said they

Table 39. Distribution of weight before the illness and in the last few weeks (Interviewer Questionnaire). Total population

Weight (lb)		<98	98–112	112–126	126–140	140–154	154–168	168–182	182–196	196–210	210 +
Before illness	Male	0	1	6	27	34	49	26	18	6	5
	Female	4	32	50	46	37	18	11	2	0	3
	Total	4	33	56	73	71	67	37	20	6	8
Last few weeks	Male	0	1	6	25	41	44	29	14	8	4
	Female	7	34	49	51	28	18	9	3	2	2
	Total	7	35	54	76	69	62	38	17	10	6

Table 40. Distributions of greatest weight ever. Total population

Weight (lb)	<98	98–112	112–126	126–140	140–154	154–168	168–182	182–196	196–210	210 +
Male	0	0	3	15	28	51	25	21	19	10
Female	1	5	45	47	43	23	24	7	5	3
Total	1	5	48	62	71	74	49	28	24	13

Table 41. Distributions of lowest adult weight. Total population

Weight (lb)	<98	98–112	112–126	126–140	140–154	154–168	168–182	182–196	196–210	210+
Male	0	4	23	54	46	26	16	2	1	0
Female	31	61	56	36	13	2	1	2	0	0
Total	31	65	79	90	59	28	17	4	1	0

Table 42. Distribution of reported weight change in the last few weeks. Total population

	Weight loss (lb.)						Weight gain (lb.)					
	10+	10–8	8–6	6–4	4–2	2–1	1–2	2–4	4–6	6–8	8–10	10+
Male	3	4	4	6	8	10	2	8	5	6	1	1
Female	4	0	9	12	16	9	1	18	11	9	0	2
Total	7	4	13	18	24	19	3	26	16	15	1	3

Table 43. Interviewer Questionnaire on weight. Distribution of consumption of psychotropic drugs by total population.

Drug	Before illness		Last few weeks	
	No	Yes	No	Yes
Tranquillizer	333	42	254	121
Sedative	343	32	280	95
Stimulant	367	8	366	9
Antidepressant	359	16	303	72
Alcohol	345	30	341	34
Heroin, cocaine, etc.	375	0	374	1
Unknown drug for "nerves"	345	30	332	43
Any	280	95	132	243
Drugs causing drowsiness	307	68	229	145

weighed themselves daily. Fifty-three patients reported weighing themselves less than once a year.

About a quarter of the population reported taking psychotropic drugs in the time before the illness compared with about two-thirds of the population in the last few weeks. Alcohol in excessive quantities is included in this list of drugs. Sixty-eight patients reported that drugs they were taking before the illness caused drowsiness, and 145 reported drowsiness due to drugs in the last few weeks (Table 43). Sixty-six patients reported suffering from co-existent physical illness. Mean measured weight was 142 ± 27 lbs. (men 156 ± 23 lbs; women 130 ± 24 lbs). The differences between mean patients' report of weight, interviewers' report of weight and measured weight are small and not statistically significant. This is of importance as it is the only area in the study in which validity of patients' and interviewers' reports can be checked against direct measurements.

The distributions of ratings by the consultants on the diagnostic category profile are displayed in Table 49. Anxiety state, personality disorder and neurotic depressive reaction were the most commonly diagnosed disorders, whilst mania, dementia and acute schizophrenia were very rare. Few patients were rated as 'very' on any diagnostic category. Additional diagnoses were rarely made and it was not regarded as necessary to give these further consideration. A very large number of different overall diagnoses was made by the consultants and it was therefore found necessary to invite an independent psychiatrist to attempt to group similar overall diagnoses together to reduce the number of categories. In this way the total number of overall diagnoses was reduced to 91. The distributions of ratings of the 12 items in Part 2 of the

Table 44. Distribution of age. Total population

Age (years)	18–25	25–30	30–35	35–40	40–45	45–50	50–55	55–60	60–65	65 +
Male	44	28	27	22	18	12	10	2	7	2
Female	64	26	32	24	12	19	11	5	2	8
Total	108	54	59	46	30	31	21	7	9	10

Table 45. Distribution of measured weight. Total population

Weight (lb)	<98	98–112	112–126	126–140	140–154	154–168	168–182	182–196	196–210	210 +
Male	0	1	11	30	42	43	23	14	3	5
Female	9	40	44	51	27	17	9	2	2	2
Total	9	41	55	81	69	60	32	16	5	7

Table 46. Distribution of triceps skinfold thickness (T.S.T.). Total population

T.S.T. (mm)	< 5	5–10	10–15	15–20	20–25	25–30	30–35	35 +
Male	7	58	52	31	17	4	2	1
Female	0	6	38	43	51	27	26	12
Total	7	64	90	74	68	31	28	13

Table 47. Distribution of subscapular skinfold thickness (S.S.T.). Total population

S.S.T. (mm)	< 5	5–10	10–15	15–20	20–25	25–30	30–35	35 +
Male	0	48	61	34	19	5	2	3
Female	2	41	55	46	30	11	3	15
Total	2	89	116	80	49	16	5	18

Table 48. Distribution of weight change since start of illness (Interviewer Questionnaire). Total population

	Weight Loss (Ib)					Weight Gain (Ib)			
	40 +	40–30	30–20	20–10	10–10	10–20	20–30	30–40	40 +
Male	0	1	5	17	128	12	6	3	0
Female	2	2	5	33	123	19	7	1	1
Total	2	3	10	50	251	31	13	4	1

Consultant Questionnaire are displayed in Table 50. Sadness, tenseness and anxiety were common, whereas elation, excitement and flatness of affect were rare. There was a striking tendency for the consultants to make lower ratings than the patients on the mood items.

Thus, overall in this population, psychiatric illness is characterized by an increase in the length of time spent in bed but a reduction in the length of time spent asleep. The reduction in the duration of sleep is contributed to by difficulty in falling asleep and interrupted sleep but not by earlier waking. Weight

Table 49. Distribution of ratings on Part 1 of Psychiatrist Questionnaire. Total population

	Not at all	Slightly	Quite a bit	Very
Conversion hysteria	281	69	23	1
Anxiety state	94	175	106	0
Obesity	328	34	10	3
Hypochondriasis	304	37	31	3
Endogenous depression	290	42	41	2
Mania	374	1	0	0
Chronic schizophrenia	361	8	5	1
Anxiety phobic state	276	59	38	2
Anorexia nervosa	360	13	2	0
Alcoholism	342	21	8	4
Addiction (other)	363	8	2	2
Psychopathy	349	15	11	0
Sexual deviation	326	16	17	16
Personality disorder (other)	192	81	95	7
Obessional state	340	26	9	0
Dementia	374	1	0	0
Neurotic depressive reaction	114	155	103	3
Paranoid state	340	20	13	2
Acute schizophrenia	371	2	1	0

Table 50. Distribution of ratings on Part 2 of Psychiatrist Questionnaire. Total population.

	Not at all	Slightly	Quite a bit	Very
Tenseness	51	213	108	1
Flatness (affect)	357	16	2	0
Agitation	332	35	7	1
Anxiety	60	215	99	1
Sadness	99	145	125	6
Elation	373	1	1	0
Weight loss	285	54	35	1
Anger	303	45	26	1
Excitement	370	5	0	0
Early morning waking	305	47	21	2
Denial	286	43	39	1

	Increased	Unchanged	Diminished	Absent
Sexual activity	10	251	76	31

change was a common feature but weight gain was almost as frequent as weight loss.

Reference

Stonehill, E., Crisp, A. H. and Koval, J. (1976). The relationship of reported sleep characteristics to psychiatric diagnosis and mood. *Br. J. med. Psychol.* (In Press)

CHAPTER 12

Study II: Weight, shape and sleep characteristics of diagnostic categories and mood states

Body weight and shape in psychiatric diagnosis

In psychiatric illness weight changes are said to be most common amongst the affective disorders. In particular marked weight loss, often superimposed on an obese body build, is said to be characteristic of endogenous depression, distinguishing it from neurotic depression.

Within this aspect of the study we have sought to explore the possibility of an association between both weight change and body shape characteristics, and the diagnoses of endogenous depression, neurotic depressive reaction and anxiety state.

Correlations between weight loss in the last few weeks and the three diagnoses were computed. There was no correlation between weight loss and endogenous depression ($r = -0.03$) or anxiety state ($r = 0.09$), but a very weak association between weight loss and neurotic depression emerged ($r = 0.15$). Weight characteristics were then examined in three groups of patients diagnosed as suffering from one of the three diagnoses. The consultants' ratings provided a profile of diagnosis (see Table 49). Thus we only included those patients who were diagnosed 'quite a bit' or 'very' on one and not more than one of the three diagnoses, endogenous depression, neurotic depressive reaction or anxiety state.

There were 21 patients diagnosed with endogenous depression, 62 with neurotic depression and 44 with anxiety state. In each of the three groups approximately half the patients reported weight loss since the start of the illness (about a third reported weight gain and the remainder no change in weight). The mean amount of weight loss in those patients who lost weight was significantly greater ($p < 0.05$) in the neurotic depression (10.3 lbs) and the anxiety state (9.61 lbs) groups than in the endogenous depression (5.4 lbs) group. There was no significant difference between the three groups in those who reported weight gain. Overall, the group with neurotic depression reported a mean weight loss of 3.0 lbs and the group with anxiety state a loss of 3.4 lbs since the start of the illness. These groups differ significantly ($p < 0.01$) from the endogenous depression group in which there was a mean weight gain of 1.3 lbs. This study has therefore not shown weight loss to be a feature of endogenous depression.

Next, the association between body shape characteristics and diagnosis was explored. There were no significant correlations within the total population of 375 patients between present Q.I. based on measured weight and height and the consultant's diagnosis of anxiety state, endogenous depression or neurotic depressive reaction. Apart from the primary disorders of weight, in which the expected correlations between Q.I. and consultant's ratings of obesity or anorexia nervosa emerged, the only diagnosis showing a weak association with present Q.I. was a negative correlation of $r = -0.15$ with the diagnosis personality disorder.

Within the total population, 43 patients were rated 'quite a bit' or 'very' for endogenous depression, 106 for neurotic depression and 146 for anxiety state (see Table 49). These groups do not exclude those in whom other diagnoses coexist, in contrast to the 'pure' groups of the previous section. The heaviest 15 per cent (by measured weight) of the total population had fewer occurrences of the diagnosis neurotic depression than the thinnest 15 per cent ($p < 0.01$) but there was no difference in the occurrence of endogenous depression or anxiety state in the two groups. Twice as many females as males were diagnosed as suffering from neurotic depression and this sex difference is likely to be a contributory factor to the negative association between body weight and neurotic depression. However, when height (a sex difference) is taken into account by calculating Q.I., the fattest third of the population still tends to show a lower occurrence of neurotic depression than the thinnest third ($p < 0.10$), but again there is no difference in the presence of endogenous depression or anxiety state in the two groups. In view of the increase that often occurs in body weight with age, it is noteworthy that the group of patients with neurotic depression is significantly thinner than the group of anxious patients despite being similar in age.

The interviewer questionnaire on weight (Tables 16 and 17) includes items on the patient's maximum (non-pregnant) and minimum adult weight ever. From these data and measured height, Quetelet's Indices of maximum and minimum body shape were calculated. Figure 39 displays the mean maximum Quetelet's Index (Q.I. maximum) and minimum Quetelet's Index (Q.I. minimum) throughout adult life, and present Q.I. based on measured weight in groups of patients diagnosed as suffering from anxiety state, endogenous depression or neurotic depression. Only patients diagnosed as suffering from one and not more than one of these diagnoses were included and the sexes are represented separately. Thus 44 patients were diagnosed as suffering exclusively from anxiety state, 21 from endogenous depression and 62 from neurotic depression. In each of the three diagnoses, females report lower Q.I. minimum than males ($p < 0.08$). This probably reflects the capacity of women in general to achieve a relatively low weight in early adult life, rooted in the wish to be slim. The males with neurotic depression had a mean lower Q.I. minimum than both the males with endogenous depression and anxiety

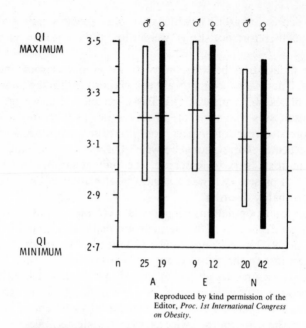

Reproduced by kind permission of the
Editor, *Proc. 1st International Congress
on Obesity.*

Figure 39. Mean maximum (Q.I. maximum) and
mean minimum (Q.I. minimum) indices of body
shape throughout adult life, and also present body
shape (—) in groups of new psychiatric out-
patients diagnosed exclusively either as anxiety state
(A), endogenous depression (E) or neurotic depression
(N) (Crisp, Stonehill and Koval, 1975)

state. The mean Q.I. maximum and the mean measured Q.I. at the time of
attendance at the clinic, for both males and females with neurotic depression
are lower than the mean values in both endogenous depression and anxiety
state. However, none of these differences achieves a 5 per cent level of
significance.

Thus we have found no evidence of a specific association between endogenous
depression and pyknic body shape measured by an index of present weight for
height and also previous maximum weight for height ever. A negative
association has been shown to exist between this measure and neurotic
depression. Patients with neurotic depression reported never having been as
'fat' as those with anxiety state or endogenous depression. Current thinness
was a feature in particular of males with neurotic depression in comparison
with the other diagnoses and this was also true of thinness in earlier adult life.

Apart from the above associations between body shape and weight and
psychiatric diagnosis, our study has shown that it is likely that major changes
in body weight during the course of a psychiatric illness depend more on
constitutional body shape characteristics of the individual than on the specific
psychiatric diagnosis. Thus, within our total population 114 patients reported
weight change of 10 lbs or more during the course of the illness, taking the

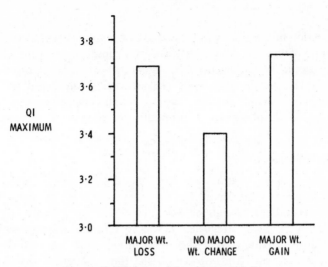

Figure 40. Major weight change (10 lb. or more) during the illness in relation to mean maximum ever index of body shape (Q.I. Maximum).

form of weight loss in 65 patients and weight gain in 49 patients. Those patients who suffered such major weight change had a significantly greater mean Q.I. maximum than those patients who did not experience major weight change during the course of the illness ($p < 0.001$) and irrespective of diagnosis. Furthermore, the Q.I. maximum was not different between those who gained 10 lbs or more and those who lost 10 lbs or more (Figure 40).

Body weight and shape in disturbed mood

The following section explores some possible associations between disturbed mood states and body weight and shape characteristics. Mood states were assessed both by the patient and by the consultant (see Chapter 10). Inspection of the distribution of mood ratings revealed that consultants tended to discriminate more than patients in their ratings of specific mood states and to provide lower ratings than the patients. Over two-thirds of patients rated themselves 'quite a bit' or 'very' nervous, sad, tense, fidgety and restless, and irritable in the last few weeks (see Table 26). This is in contrast to the consultant's ratings of feeling in which the category 'very' was seldom selected (Table 50). The tendency for higher self-ratings by patients, compared with the ratings of them by the consultants, may reflect the more subjective frame of reference used by the patient when measuring his own unpleasant feelings, as opposed to the clinician's tendency to rate him in comparison to others. The clinician's approach, in which an attempt to make a discrete diagnosis incorporates the careful examination, and, as far as possible, the separation of disturbed mood states, probably also accounts to some extent for the greater discrimination between mood states displayed by the consultants.

In this section no specific hypotheses have been tested except the proposition that the state of sadness which often forms a central core in the diagnosis of depression would be expected to be associated with the greatest degree of weight loss. The weight and shape characteristics considered are the same as those in the previous section, namely weight change during the illness, and Quetelet's Index of maximum, minimum and present body shape.

Patients' ratings of mood

It was not possible to examine 'pure' mood states, e.g. a rating of 'very' sad in the absence of similar ratings on other moods, as the patients did not generally discriminate enough between the moods to provide large enough numbers for such 'pure' categories. It was therefore decided to compare two global categories, namely 'very disturbed mood' and 'less disturbed mood'. The less disturbed mood group comprised those patients who did not rate themselves high (mood rating of less than 'very') on any of the following six moods in the last few weeks: nervous, sad, tense, fidgety and restless, and irritable. This category includes 101 patients (50 males, 51 females). The very disturbed mood group includes those who rated themselves as 'very' on any three or more of these moods and comprises 121 patients (44 males, 77 females). Thus, each group included about a third of the total population. Ratings of on top of the world and excited were excluded on the basis that they were usually not regarded by the patients as unpleasant or disturbed moods.

The two groups do not differ in respect of age, Q.I. maximum or present Q.I. They are, however, distinguished in respect of Q.I. minimum. The very disturbed mood group is found to have been significantly thinner ($p < 0.01$) than the less disturbed mood group (Figure 41). The two groups are not different in respect of major weight gain (10 lbs or more) since the start of the illness.

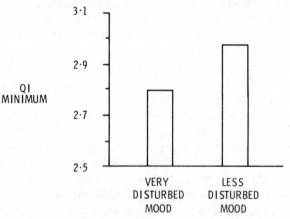

Figure 41. Patients' rating of disturbed mood during illness in relation to minimum adult index of body shape (Q.I. minimum)

However the very disturbed mood group has a significantly higher incidence of major weight loss (10 lbs or more) since the start of the illness than the less disturbed mood group ($p < 0.02$). One possible factor contributing to the mean lower Q.I. minimum in the very disturbed mood group is that of sex, for the very disturbed group contains a preponderance of females. However, this does not apply to weight loss, since the males with very disturbed mood had a significantly greater mean weight loss ($p < 0.02$) than the males with less disturbed mood.

Consultants' ratings of mood

In the case of consultants' ratings of mood, it proved possible to produce discrete categories of the moods tense, anxious, sad and angry. This was accomplished by including only those patients who were rated as having the presence of one and only one of these moods and excluding all patients in whom more than one of the rated mood states were judged to be present. Inevitably this gave rise to rather small groups and it is a possible consequence of this that few statistically significant differences emerged. There were no

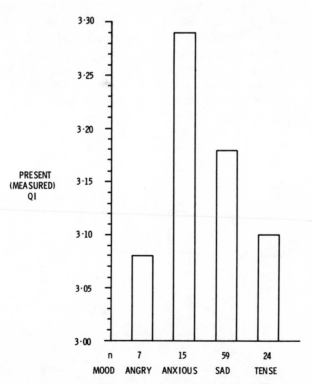

Figure 42. Present Quetelet's Index (Q.I.) in relation to consultants' ratings of moods

124

striking differences between the moods in relation to Q.I. maximum. Figure 42 displays in histogram form the relation between present Q.I. and the four discrete moods. Numbers in the anxious and angry categories are small. There is, nevertheless, a tendency for the mood angry and the mood tense to be associated with a greater degree of current thinness than the mood anxious and the mood sad. This difference becomes more striking if the female population is examined separately, when the present Q.I. in the tense and angry group becomes significantly lower ($p < 0.05$) than the sad and anxious groups. The relative thinness of these two groups is further confirmed by their lower triceps skinfold thickness scores ($p < 0.05$) and sub-scapular skinfold thickness scores ($p < 0.02$).

Figure 43 displays Q.I. in relation to the four moods. There is a tendency for patients rated as tense by the consultant to have had a lower Q.I. maximum, i.e. never to have been as fat as patients rated angry, anxious or sad. Thus tension but not sadness is a mood seemingly associated with the absence of previous or current obesity. It will be remembered from the previous section that the diagnosis neurotic depression, in which tension is usually a clinical feature, seemed to be associated with these body shape characteristics and it is noteworthy that sadness does not seem to be similarly associated.

The four mood groups do not appear different in respect of major weight gain (10 lbs or more). However, there was a trend ($p < 0.10$) for the incidence of major weight loss (10 lbs or more) since the start of the illness to be greater in both the tense and the sad groups, than in the angry and anxious groups. The finding of an association between weight loss and sadness is an expected one, and although the expected association between shape characteristics and sadness failed to emerge, the constitutional body shape features of tension and the association of weight loss with both tension and sadness fit with the earlier findings that these nutritional characteristics typify the diagnosis of neurotic depression.

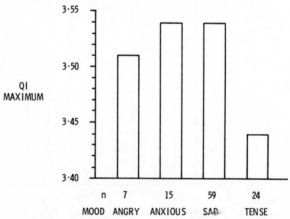

Figure 43. Index of maximum body shape ever (Q.I. maximum) in relation to consultants' ratings of moods

Sleep Characteristics of Psychiatric Diagnostic Categories

Sleep disturbance is said to be most common in affective illness. In particular, endogenous depression is said to be characterized by major insomnia, associated especially with early morning waking but not with difficulty in falling asleep. This is in contrast to neurotic depression which is said to be associated with initial insomnia but no special tendency to early waking.

The study provides support for the view that reduction of sleep characterizes psychiatric illness. Thus, within the total population the average duration of sleep before the illness was 7 hours 16 minutes and this differs little from the average duration of sleep in the general population. Whereas the average duration of sleep in the last few weeks was 6 hours 52 minutes and this is a reduction of 24 minutes compared with before the illness ($p < 0.005$). Psychiatric illness was not characterized by a difference in the time of going to bed compared with before the illness, but it was characterized by an increased time in falling asleep. The time taken to fall asleep rose from 31 minutes before the illness to 51 minutes on average in the last few weeks and this difference is significant ($p < 0.005$). Thus, a general psychiatric population is characterized by a delayed onset of sleep. The mean duration of wakefulness in the night, after first falling asleep and before final waking (broken sleep) was 9 minutes before the illness and 20 minutes in the last few weeks, and the association between increased broken sleep and psychiatric illness is statistically significant ($p < 0.001$).

The average time of waking in the morning was not significantly different before the illness and in the last few weeks although in common with many sleep items there was a large variance. Overall, therefore, early morning waking is not a characteristic of this population. It should be mentioned, however, that 91 patients reported the regular consumption of hypnotics in the last few weeks compared with only 29 patients before the illness. In summary therefore, the present psychiatric population is characterized by a total reduction in its duration of sleep contributed to by difficulty in falling asleep and interrupted sleep but not by alteration in the time of waking in the morning.

Within the affective disorders the present study has provided an opportunity to make a comparison of the sleep patterns of the three diagnostic categories often thought to be characterized by distinctive sleep disturbance, namely anxiety state, endogenous depression and neurotic depression. This report concerns those patients who were diagnosed 'quite a bit' or 'very' on one and not more than one of these three diagnoses, thereby once more providing three groups each with a 'pure' diagnosis. Thus, those patients who for example were regarded as displaying features of both endogenous depression and neurotic depression were again excluded.

It had been established that two of the consultants supported the view of the independent existence of endogenous depression and neurotic depression, whereas the other two consultants supported the continuum view of depression. This difference was not felt to be important as the psychiatrists' diagnostic questionnaire imposed the distinction between endogenous depression and neurotic depression on the consultants. It was nevertheless considered worth-while to invite the consultants to describe their view of the sleep characteristics of the three diagnoses. Although there were some differences in emphasis between the consultants, on the whole they did not make a marked distinction between sleep in anxiety state and neurotic depression, in both of which difficulty falling asleep was regarded as a major characteristic. This was in contrast to their view of endogenous depression in which difficulty falling asleep was sometimes regarded as a feature but in which early morning waking was seen as a major characteristic. Broken sleep was felt to be sometimes important in all three diagnoses but did not on the whole distinguish between the diagnoses.

Forty-four patients were diagnosed exclusively as suffering from anxiety state, 21 from endogenous depression and 62 from neurotic depression. Figure 44 displays the average duration of sleep in the three diagnoses. This was similar in anxiety state and endogenous depression, being 7 hours 7 minutes and 7 hours 8 minutes respectively. This is somewhat longer than the average duration of sleep in the total population which was 6 hours and 52 minutes. The average duration of sleep in neurotic depression was 6 hours 18 minutes and this is significantly less than in the total population ($p < 0.01$), and also significantly less than in endogenous depression or anxiety state ($p < 0.05$). Thus the greatest amount of overall sleep disturbance is evident in neurotic depression.

Patients with endogenous depression also reported going to bed earlier (11.0 p.m.) than patients with anxiety state (11.26 p.m.) and neurotic depression (11.28 p.m.), but these differences do not reach statistical significance. Patients

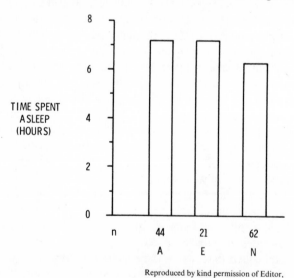

Reproduced by kind permission of Editor,
Br. J. med. Psychol.

Figure 44. Average duration of sleep in anxiety state (A), endogenous depression (E) and neurotic depression (N)
(Stonehill, Crisp and Koval, 1976)

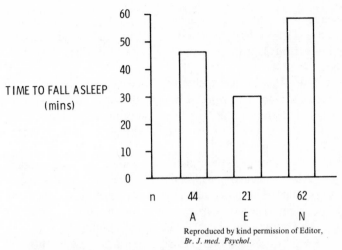

TIME TO FALL ASLEEP (mins)

Figure 45. Average time taken to fall asleep in anxiety state
(A), endogenous depression (E) and neurotic depression (N)
(Stonehill, Crisp and Koval, 1976)

with endogenous depression fell asleep after 30 minutes on average and this
delay in falling asleep is significantly less than in the total population ($p < 0.05$)
in which the mean was 53 minutes. The time taken to fall asleep was longer
in anxiety state and in neurotic depression, it being 47 minutes and 58 minutes
respectively (Figure 45). On average patients with endogenous depression
reported falling asleep at 11.41 p.m. whereas patients with anxiety state and
neurotic depression fell asleep at 12.12 a.m. and 12.27 a.m. respectively.

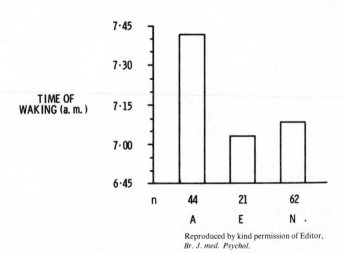

Figure 46. Average time of waking in anxiety state (A),
endogenous depression (E) and neurotic depression (N)
(Stonehill, Crisp and Koval, 1976)

The average amount of broken sleep in endogenous depression was 14 minutes and this is less than in anxiety state and neurotic depression in which it was 22 minutes and 23 minutes respectively but this does not reach statistical significance.

Finally (Figure 46), the average time of waking up in endogenous depression and neurotic depression was similar, being 7.03 a.m. and 7.08 a.m. respectively. This is earlier than the average for the total population which was 7.19 a.m., but patients with anxiety state reported waking significantly later than this, namely at 7.42 a.m. ($p < 0.05$).

In summary, of the three diagnostic categories, the least average duration of sleep was present in neurotic depression. This latter condition is characterized by going to bed late. The short duration of sleep is contributed to by the delay in falling asleep, interrupted sleep and early waking. Endogenous depression is characterized by going to bed early, falling asleep quickly, a small amount of interrupted sleep but early waking. Early waking is not a feature which distinguished endogenous depression from neurotic depression, but it did distinguish both these syndromes from anxiety state.

Sleep Characteristics of Disturbed Mood

The preceding section has drawn attention to an overall reduction in the total duration of sleep, characterized by delayed onset of sleep and increased broken sleep in association with depressed mood, which is a feature of psychiatric illness.

Patients' ratings of mood

The first component of the principal components analysis (see Chapter 13), which accounted for 12.8 per cent of the variance, comprised patients' ratings of all the unpleasant feelings rated in association with taking longer to fall asleep. In addition, it also included the need to be wakened. Thus this adds substance to the view that unpleasant affect is associated only with difficulty falling asleep. In contrast, total sleep reduction was not a feature of this component and furthermore the need to be wakened implies that disturbed mood may be associated with a forward shift of the total sleep period.

The association between sleep characteristics and patients' report of disturbed mood was further examined in respect of the two categories 'very disturbed mood' and 'less disturbed mood' already described in the second section of this chapter. Time of going to bed was not different in the two groups, being 11.15 p.m. in the less disturbed group and 11.20 p.m. in the very disturbed group. The very disturbed group is characterized, however, by taking 24 minutes longer to fall asleep than the less disturbed group and consequently the time of falling asleep in the former group is significantly later (12.24 a.m.) than in the latter group in which it was 11.55 p.m. ($p < 0.02$). The amount of broken sleep in the very disturbed group is also significantly greater ($p < 0.02$) than in the less disturbed group, being 60 minutes and 25 minutes respectively. Time of waking was not, however, different between the two groups, the disturbed group having a total sleep time of 6 hours 28 minutes, which is significantly less (p < 0.02) than the less disturbed group in which it was 7 hours 1 minute. These findings, therefore, confirm the selective impact of disturbed mood on sleep as being in the first part of the night.

Psychiatrists' ratings of mood

As in the second section of this chapter, the psychiatrists' emphasis on discriminating between the various disturbed mood states enabled us to examine sleep characteristics in relation to the discrete mood states angry, anxious, sad and tense. Within some of these categories numbers were small and the variance of sleep items tended to be large. However, it is considered worthwhile to mention some of the trends. Figure 47 displays the average duration of sleep within the four groups. The least amount of total sleep occurred in the angry group and was 6 hours 9 minutes, and this is nearly an hour less than in the tense and anxious groups in which it was 6 hours 52 minutes and 6 hours 58 minutes respectively. The sad group slept on average for 6 hours 39 minutes. Figure 48 shows the average time of going to bed in the groups. The tense group went to bed latest at nearly midnight (11.53 p.m.), whereas the sad and anxious groups went to bed considerably earlier (11.11 p.m. and 11.12 p.m. respectively). Initial insomnia (Figure 49) was greatest in the anxious group, being 73 minutes, and least in the tense group in which it was 41 minutes. Broken sleep (Figure 50) was greatest in the angry group in which it averaged 44 minutes and least in the tense group in which it was 19 minutes. Finally, average time of waking was earliest in the sad group (7.17 a.m.) and latest in the anxious group (7.58 a.m.) (Figure 51). Overall, the mood of anger seems to be characterized by sleep disturbance throughout the night, anxious mood by initial insomnia, broken

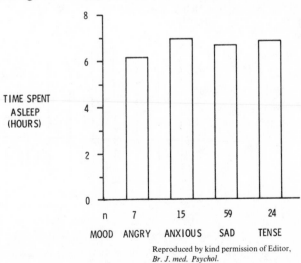

Reproduced by kind permission of Editor,
Br. J. med. Psychol.

Figure 47. Average duration of sleep in relation to
consultants' ratings of moods
(Stonehill, Crisp and Koval, 1976)

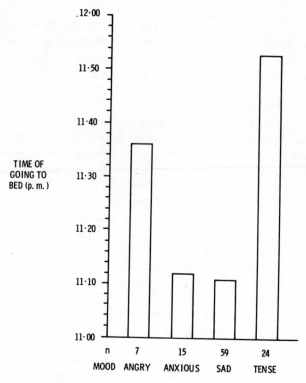

Figure 48. Average time of going to bed in relation to
consultants' ratings of moods
(Stonehill, Crisp and Koval, 1976)

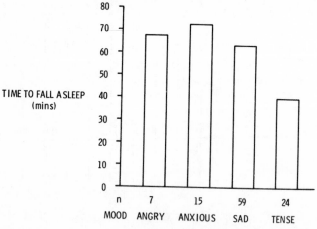

Figure 49. Average time taken to fall asleep in relation
to consultants' ratings of moods
(Stonehill, Crisp and Koval, 1976)

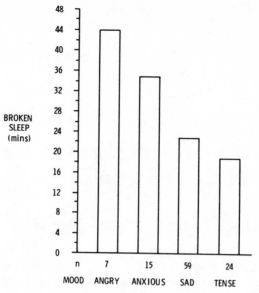

Figure 50. Average amount of broken sleep in
relation to consultants' ratings of moods
(Stonehill, Crisp and Koval, 1976)

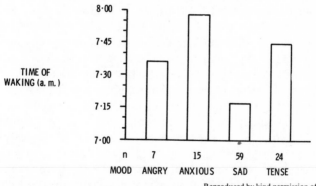

Figure 51. Average time of waking in relation to consultants' ratings of moods
(Stonehill, Crisp and Koval, 1976)

sleep but delayed waking in the morning, sadness by going to bed early with some delayed onset of sleep but strikingly with early waking, and tension only by going to bed late.

References

Crisp, A. H., Stonehill, E. and Koval, J. (1975). The pyknic habitus in psychiatric illness, In (Ed. Howard, A.) Recent Advances in Obesity Research: 1, London, Newman Publishing, pp. 199–201.

Stonehill, E., Crisp, A. H. and Koval, J. (1976). The relationship of reported sleep characteristics to psychiatric diagnosis and mood. *Br. J. med. Psychol.* (In Press)

CHAPTER 13

Study II: The relationship between weight and sleep in the total population

A. Intercorrelations and Principle Components Analysis

An intercorrelational matrix was prepared between most single items of information as well as some items derived from two or more single items on the total population. Intercorrelations between 30 items selected to include a cross section of information about nutrition, sleep, mood and psychiatric diagnosis, were submitted to a principle components analysis. Items of interviewers' information were used where data were available on both patients' and interviewers' information as the latter included more aspects of sleep and the two types of data were anyway very highly correlated. Table 51 displays the 30 items together with their loadings on the first 10 principle components after varima rotation. As expected no single major component emerged.

Components 1, 2, 4, 6 and 7 contain high loadings in only one of the three areas of sleep, nutrition and psychiatric state. Component 3 reveals a weak association between increase in broken sleep, diminished total sleep, length of time in bed in the last few weeks and weight loss in the last few weeks. Thus this component shows a weak association between recent weight loss and disturbed sleep, independent of disturbed mood or psychiatric diagnosis. Component 5 comprised increased duration of sleep, particularly later waking but also later time of falling asleep, together with weight gain since the start of the illness but particularly in the last few weeks. Component 8 shows an association between delayed falling asleep, spontaneous waking in the morning, the consumption of sleeping pills and a weak link with loss of weight, independent of psychiatric status. Component 9 reveals a weak link between patients' ratings of 'feeling on top of the world' and 'feeling excited' with the consumption of sleeping pills and earlier time of falling asleep. Finally component 10 includes the diagnosis of endogenous depression and the consultant's rating of sadness as well as falling asleep more quickly and waking spontaneously, but not weight change, change in duration of sleep or patients' rating of sadness.

Thus components 3, 5 and 8 demonstrate a link between weight change and change in sleep distributed throughout the night. Weight loss is associated with decreased sleep, and weight gain with increased sleep, independent of mood ratings by the patients, or the consultant psychiatrist's diagnosis.

Table 51. Thirty-item principal components analysis. Loadings on first 10 components. Total population (Crisp and Stonehill, 1973)

30 items	Rotated component loadings and % variance									
	1 (12.8)	2 (8.6)	3 (6.7)	4 (6.4)	5 (5.9)	6 (5.5)	7 (4.8)	8 (4.5)	9 (3.9)	10 (3.7)
Weight loss since start of illness (interviewers' report)	.07	.06	.11	−.52	−.25	.08	.09	.22	−.11	−.05
Weight loss in last few weeks	.09	.03	.27	−.24	−.43	−.03	.04	.22	.01	.09
Triceps skinfold thickness	.04	−.10	.00	.78	.01	−.02	.09	.04	−.12	.06
Subscapular skinfold thickness	−.09	−.01	.11	.50	−.08	.11	.10	−.17	.07	−.02
Quetelet's index (from measured weight and height)	−.10	−.01	−.02	.79	−.05	−.06	−.10	.12	−.02	.07
Recently going to bed later than before illness (interviewers' report)	−.02	.81	.03	−.15	.08	.04	.04	−.27	.05	.12
Recently taking longer to fall asleep than before illness (interviewers' report)	.20	.26	.15	.15	.11	.04	−.05	.65	−.24	−.36
Recent length of time asleep less than before illness (interviewers' report)	.13	.71	.28	−.01	−.44	.05	.00	.13	−.06	−.06
Greater duration of broken sleep recently than before illness	.06	.02	.87	.00	.01	.05	.02	.02	−.01	.04
Length of time in bed in last few weeks (interviewers' report)	−.01	−.62	.35	.03	.41	.07	−.03	.32	−.14	−.07
Number of sleep interruptions in last few weeks	.10	−.02	.83	.03	.00	.00	.11	.07	−.04	−.03
Need to be wakened in last few weeks	.22	.08	−.16	.16	.10	−.02	−.11	−.58	.00	−.20
Sleeping pills in last few weeks	.04	−.11	−.05	−.07	−.10	.01	.11	.56	.21	.04
Time of waking in last few weeks (interviewers' report)	.01	.04	.12	−.09	.91	.00	−.07	−.03	.03	−.04
Time of falling asleep in last few weeks (interviewers' report)	.16	.80	−.09	−.06	.30	.01	.00	.28	−.01	−.17
Feeling nervous in last few weeks (patients' rating)	.57	−.18	.08	−.09	−.06	.40	.06	.07	−.05	.00
Feeling angry in last few weeks (patients' rating)	.61	.13	.02	−.05	.11	−.04	.21	−.05	.13	.04

Table 51. (*Contd.*)

30 items	Rotated component loadings and % variance									
	1 (12.8)	2 (8.6)	3 (6.7)	4 (6.4)	5 (5.9)	6 (5.5)	7 (4.8)	8 (4.5)	9 (3.9)	10 (3.7)
Feeling on top of the world in last few weeks (patients' rating)	-.12	.02	-.03	-.04	-.01	-.05	-.06	-.05	.77	-.09
Feeling excited in last few weeks (patients' rating)	.23	.04	-.03	.07	.05	.15	-.10	.17	.75	-.08
Feeling sad in last few weeks (patients' rating)	.60	-.01	.01	.03	.12	-.11	.34	.15	.11	.09
Feeling tense in last few weeks (patients' rating)	.70	.00	.04	-.06	-.06	.21	.06	.01	-.17	-.03
Feeling fidgety and restless in last few weeks (patients' rating)	.61	.15	.08	-.08	-.12	.08	-.12	-.04	.08	.00
Feeling irritable in last few weeks (patients' rating)	.79	.01	.02	-.01	-.03	-.11	.07	-.02	-.05	-.04
Diagnosis of anxiety state	.07	.00	-.02	-.04	-.04	.83	.11	.08	-.01	.01
Diagnosis of endogenous depression	.11	.03	.01	.08	-.06	-.04	.12	.00	-.16	.80
Diagnosis of anxiety phobic state	.02	-.05	.02	.12	-.07	.66	-.15	-.13	.06	-.10
Diagnosis of personality disorder	.18	.07	-.01	-.11	.02	-.07	.46	-.12	.03	-.52
Diagnosis of neurotic depressive reaction	.16	.00	.11	.00	-.11	.16	.79	.09	-.09	-.15
Tenseness (psychiatrists' rating)	.01	.16	.04	-.09	.18	.59	.20	.09	.03	.10
Sadness (psychiatrists' rating)	.16	.01	.06	.08	-.05	.05	.79	.15	-.14	.30

Reproduced by kind permission of the Editor, *British Journal of Psychiatry*.

Components 1 and 9 show a link between patients' ratings of feelings and changes in sleep limited to the beginning of the night. Thus unpleasant feelings are associated with taking longer to fall asleep, and 'feeling on top of the world' and 'feeling excited' with falling asleep more quickly.

B. 2 × 2 Contingency Tables

Relationships between various aspects of sleep and nutritional status in different psychiatric states were explored by the formation and analysis of a series of 2 × 2 contingency tables. In the light of the traditionally held view of the association of both weight changes and sleep disturbance with affective disorders, psychiatric diagnoses in the areas of depression and anxiety and feelings of sadness were selected for examination, so that the relationship between aspects of nutrition and sleep could be examined in each of them. The specific states chosen for such examination in most cases are displayed in Table 52 and include all subjects rated 'quite a bit' or 'very' as distinct from

Table 52. 2 × 2 Contingency Table. The relationship between length of time asleep in the last few weeks (Interviewer Questionnaire) and weight change in the last few weeks in different psychiatric states

Diagnosis and state of sadness	Wt. change in last few weeks	Length of Time asleep (hr) $< 6\frac{1}{2}$ $> 7\frac{1}{2}$		X^2	p*
Endogenous depression and/or neurotic depressive reaction	Wt. loss Wt. gain	30 10	6 12	7.47	< 0.005
Endogenous depression	Wt. loss Wt. gain	7 2	2 5	Fisher test	N.S. (< 0.10)
Neurotic depressive reaction	Wt. loss Wt. gain	26 8	4 7	4.38	< 0.02
No endogenous depression or neurotic depressive reaction	Wt. loss Wt. gain	20 11	17 18	1.70	N.S. (< 0.10)
Anxiety state and/or anxiety phobic state	Wt. loss Wt. gain	16 5	8 10	2.87	< 0.05
Depression included in overall diagnosis	Wt. loss Wt. gain	31 10	5 11	7.95	< 0.002
Sad in last few weeks (Patient Questionaire)	Wt. loss Wt. gain	38 14	17 18	4.41	< 0.02
Sadness (Psychiatrist Questionnaire)	Wt. loss Wt. gain	26 10	7 9	2.74	< 0.05

* = one-tail test

'not at all' and 'slightly' in each instance. It was recognized that in some tables numbers would be rather small, and on this account, for instance, 'endogenous depression and/or neurotic depressive reaction' are included together as well as separately.

Table 52 displays the relationship between length of time asleep in the last few weeks (Interviewer Questionnaire) and recent weight change in the selected psychiatric states. A significant association between weight loss and length of sleep of $6\frac{1}{2}$ hours or less, and between weight gain and length of sleep of $7\frac{1}{2}$ hours or more, was demonstrated in all psychiatric states except 'endogenous depression', where the tendency was in the same direction but the numbers small, and in the category 'no endogenous depression or neurotic depressive reaction', where the same trend nevertheless still existed. Moreover, when the category 'endogenous depression' was combined with that of 'neurotic depressive reaction', the statistical significance of the relationship between weight change and duration of sleep became greater ($p < 0.005$) than in neurotic depressive reaction alone ($p < 0.02$). This table also shows that the link between duration of sleep and weight change is strongest in psychiatric states in which depression is diagnosed, and less strong in 'anxiety states', 'patients' rating of sadness' and 'psychiatrist's rating of sadness'. When the mean age of patients sleeping $6\frac{1}{2}$ hours or less is compared with that of patients sleeping $7\frac{1}{2}$ hours or more in each of the categories, there is no significant difference in any instance. When patient report is substituted for interviewer report in the states 'endogenous depression and/or neurotic depressive reaction', 'depression included in the overall diagnosis', and 'patients' rating of sadness', the findings remain very similar (Table 53).

When patients who reported that they were taking psychotropic drugs causing drowsiness (Table 43) or who were suffering from co-existent physical illness (possibly affecting sleep) were excluded, the relationship between

Table 53. 2×2 Contingency Table. The relationship between length of time asleep in the last few weeks (Patient Questionnaire) and weight change in the last few weeks in different psychiatric states

Diagnosis and state of sadness	Wt. change in last few weeks	Length of time asleep (hr) $< 6\frac{1}{2}$ > $7\frac{1}{2}$		X^2	p^*
Endogenous depression and/or neurotic depressive reaction	Wt. loss Wt. gain	29 8	7 12	7.71	< 0.005
Depression included in overall diagnosis	Wt. loss Wt. gain	32 12	6 12	6.78	< 0.005
Sad in last few weeks (patient rating)	Wt. loss Wt. gain	36 14	16 19	4.95	< 0.02

$* =$ one-tail test

Table 54. 2 × 2 Contingency Table. The relationship between length of time asleep in the last few weeks (Interviewer Questionnaire) and weight change in the last few weeks in different psychiatric states in patients not taking drugs causing drowsiness and not suffering from coexistent physical illness

Diagnosis and state of sadness	Wt. change in last few weeks	Length of time asleep (hr) $< 6\frac{1}{2}$	$> 7\frac{1}{2}$	X^2	p^*
Endogenous depression and/or neurotic depressive reaction	Wt. loss Wt. gain	12 5	1 6	Fisher test	< 0.02
No endogenous depression or neurotic depressive reaction	Wt. loss Wt. gain	8 8	5 8	0.39	N.S.
Depression included in overall diagnosis	Wt. loss Wt. gain	12 5	1 5	Fisher test	< 0.05
Sad in last few weeks (Patient Questionnaire)	Wt. loss Wt. gain	18 11	2 9	4.51	< 0.02

* = one-tail test

Table 55. 2 × 2 Contingency Table. The relationship of change in length of time asleep between the last few weeks and before illness (Interviewer Questionnaire) and weight change in the last few weeks in patients not suffering from endogenous depression or neurotic depressive reaction who were not taking drugs causing drowsiness or suffering from coexistent physical illness

Diagnosis	Wt. change in last few weeks	Length of time asleep in last few weeks compared with before illness (min.) > 30 less	> 30 more	X^2	p^*
No endogenous depression or neurotic depressive reaction.	Wt. loss Wt. gain	12 8	2 8	2.83	< 0.05

* = one-tail test

weight and sleep remained the same except in the category 'no endogenous depression or neurotic depressive reaction (Table 54). In this category, however, a significant relationship emerged between weight loss and reduction in the duration of sleep of 30 minutes or more than before the illness, and conversely between weight gain and an increase in sleep of 30 minutes or more than before the illness (Table 55).

Within the study we also attempted to assess the impact of the consumption of a drink or snack on sleep characteristics. One hundred and twenty-seven subjects reported that they had not usually taken a drink or snack before going to bed in the last few weeks compared with 235 subjects who said that they had usually taken refreshment. In the light of the hypothesized association between nutrition and sleep, it was thought to be important to compare these two groups in respect of their reported sleep characteristics. It was recognized however, that the impact of psychotropic drugs, which were being taken by a large number of patients, might mask any association between drinks or snacks and sleep, and therefore all those patients who reported taking tranquillizers, sedatives, stimulants, antidepressants, alcohol, heroin or cocaine, unknown drug for nerves or drugs causing drowsiness were excluded, and this reduced the numbers of those taking a drink or snack to 47 and those not taking a drink or snack to 82. The two groups were similar in their age and sex distributions and in respect of their measured Q.I. There was no significant difference between the two groups when they were compared in respect of the following characteristics during the last few weeks: time of going to bed, time of falling asleep, time of waking up, time of getting up and amount of broken sleep. Although the difference in the amount of broken sleep between the two groups did not reach statistical significance because the variance was high, there was a trend in the predicted direction for the amount of broken sleep to be less in the group taking a drink or snack (12.4 ± 28 minutes) than in the group taking no drink or snack in which it was 19.1 ± 42 minutes.

When duration of sleep was explored in relation to the full range of patients' feeling states rated 'quite a bit' or 'very' (Patient Questionnaire), it was found that the association already demonstrated between weight loss and sleeping $6\frac{1}{2}$ hours or less, and between weight gain and sleeping $7\frac{1}{2}$ hours or more in the state of sadness, was also present in each of the other states, except for those concerned with elation in which numbers were small (Table 56).

Table 57 displays the relationship between time of waking and weight change in the last few weeks in the selected psychiatric states. A significant association between weight loss and early morning waking (waking before 6.30 a.m.), and between weight gain and waking after 7.30 a.m. was demonstrated in the states of sadness and all diagnoses except 'endogenous depression' ($p < 0.10$), 'neurotic depressive reaction' ($p < 0.10$) and 'anxiety state' ($p < 0.10$). However, once again when the categories of 'endogenous depression' and 'neurotic depressive reaction' are combined, the relationship between weight change and time of waking becomes significant ($p < 0.05$). Whereas Table 52 shows that the relationship between weight change and duration of sleep failed to reach significance at the 5 per cent level in patients diagnosed as not suffering from depression, Table 57 reveals a significant relationship ($p < 0.01$) between weight change and time of waking in this psychiatric state. Age was not found to be a factor, for when the mean age of patients waking at 6.30 a.m. or before is compared with the mean age of patients waking at 7.30 a.m. or later, there is no significant difference in any instance. Once more when patients' report

Table 56. 2 × 2 Contingency Table. The relationship between length of time asleep in the last few weeks (Interviewer Questionnaire) and weight change in the last few weeks in different feeling states (Patient Questionnaire)

Feeling state	Wt. change in last few weeks	Length of time asleep (hr) $< 6\frac{1}{2}$ $> 7\frac{1}{2}$		X^2	p*
Nervous	Wt. loss	44	20	3.63	< 0.05
	Wt. gain	17	19		
Angry	Wt. loss	20	9	2.82	< 0.05
	Wt. gain	8	12		
On top of the world	Wt. loss	8	2	Fisher test	N.S.
	Wt. gain	4	3		
Excited	Wt. loss	14	7	Fisher test	N.S.
	Wt. gain	5	4		
Tense	Wt. loss	47	22	4.71	< 0.02
	Wt. gain	18	22		
Fidgety and restless	Wt. loss	39	20	3.97	< 0.02
	Wt. gain	16	21		
Irritable	Wt. loss	37	17	3.08	< 0.05
	Wt. gain	15	17		

* = one-tail test

was substituted for interviewers' report in the combined category 'endogenous depression and/or neurotic depressive reaction', 'depression included in the overall diagnosis' and 'patients' rating of sadness', the findings are very similar to the corresponding findings based on interviewers' report (Table 57). Together with similar evidence displayed in Table 53, this provides further confirmation of the close association between patients' and interviewers' reports justifying the use of single measures of these items in the contingency tables. When time of waking was restricted to those patients who reported waking spontaneously in two groups of subjects, one group reporting themselves as more sad and the other group as unchanged in this respect in the last few weeks compared with before the illness, then a significant relationship between weight loss and earlier waking and between weight gain and later waking was demonstrated in both groups, especially in those who had become more sad (Table 58).

Table 59 displays the relationship between time of falling asleep and weight change in the last few weeks in each of the diagnoses and the state of sadness. It was decided to compare patients falling asleep after 1.00 a.m. with those falling asleep at 11.30 p.m. or earlier, thus excluding just over a third of the total population about the mean which was 12.07 a.m. No significant association

Table 57. 2 × 2 Contingency Table. The relationship between time of waking in the last few weeks (Interviewer Questionnaire) and weight changes in the last few weeks in different psychiatric states

Diagnosis and state of sadness	Wt. change in last few weeks	Time of waking (a.m.) < 6.30 > 7.30		X^2	p*
Endogenous depression and/or neurotic depressive reaction	Wt. loss Wt. gain	22 6	10 11	3.82	< 0.05
Endogenous depression	Wt. loss Wt. gain	8 2	1 3	Fisher test	N.S. (< 0.10)
Neurotic depressive reaction	Wt. loss Wt. gain	17 4	9 8	2.24	N.S. (< 0.10)
No endogenous depression or neurotic depressive reaction	Wt. loss Wt. gain	16 4	20 26	6.14	< 0.01
Anxiety state and/or anxiety phobic state	Wt. loss Wt. gain	13 3	9 8	1.86	N.S. (< 0.10)
Depression included in overall diagnosis	Wt. loss Wt. gain	21 6	11 11	3.01	< 0.05
Sad in last few weeks (Patient Questionnaire)	Wt. loss Wt. gain	26 5	22 27	10.45	< 0.002
Sadness (Psychiatrist Questionnaire)	Wt. loss Wt. gain	20 5	10 10	3.28	< 0.05

* = one-tail test

Table 58. 2 × 2 Contingency Table. The relationship of change in time between spontaneous waking in the last few weeks and before the illness (Patient Questionnaire) and weight change in the last few weeks in two psychiatric states

State of sadness	Wt. change in last few weeks	Spontaneous waking in last few weeks > 30 min. earlier > 30 min. later		X^2	p*
More sad in last few weeks Patient Q'aire)	Wt. loss Wt. gain	12 0	4 9	Fisher test	< 0.005
Sadness unchanged (Patient Q'aire)	Wt. loss Wt. gain	12 3	7 9	2.94	< 0.05

* = one-tail test

Table 59 2 × 2 Contingency Table. The relationship between time of falling asleep in the last few weeks (Interviewer Questionnaire) and weight change in the last few weeks in different psychiatric states

Diagnosis and state	Wt. change in last few weeks	Time of falling asleep		X^2	p
		< 11.30 p.m.	> 1.00 a.m.		
Endogenous depression and/or neurotic depressive reaction	Wt. loss Wt. gain	13 5	13 10	1.07	N.S.
Endogenous depression	Wt. loss Wt. gain	5 2	2 3	Fisher test	N.S.
Neurotic depressive reaction	Wt. loss Wt. gain	8 3	12 7	Fisher test	N.S.
No endogenous depression or neurotic depressive reaction	Wt. loss Wt. gain	16 18	14 11	0.46	N.S.
Anxiety state and/or anxiety phobic state	Wt. loss Wt. gain	13 9	7 5	0.00	N.S.
Depression included in overall diagnosis	Wt. loss Wt. gain	12 6	11 9	0.54	N.S.
Sad in last few weeks (Patient questionnaire)	Wt. loss Wt. gain	20 11	20 17	0.76	N.S.
Sadness (Psychiatrist Questionnaire)	Wt. loss Wt. gain	12 5	12 9	0.73	N.S.

between weight change and time of falling asleep emerged in any of the psychiatric diagnoses or the state of sadness.

The relationship between broken sleep and weight change in the last few weeks in each of the psychiatric diagnoses and the state of sadness, is displayed in Table 60. The number of patients without broken sleep could not be determined from the distribution table (Table 31, Chapter 11) which grouped the absence of broken sleep together with sleep broken for up to 15 minutes. About a quarter of the population reported broken sleep of 30 minutes or more, and this group was compared with patients reporting no broken sleep. A significant association between weight loss and the presence of broken sleep and between weight gain and the absence of broken sleep was demonstrated in 'neurotic depressive reaction' ($p < 0.05$), 'endogenous depression and/or neurotic depressive reaction' ($p < 0.05$) and 'patients' rating of sadness' ($p < 0.02$). No significant relationship between broken sleep and weight change emerged in 'endogenous depression' (small numbers), 'the absence of

Table 60. 2 × 2 Contingency Table. The relationship between broken sleep in the last few weeks and weight change in the last few weeks in different psychiatric states

Diagnosis and state of sadness	Wt. change in last few weeks	Duration of broken sleep (min.)		X^2	p^{**}
		0 >	30		
Endogenous depression and/or neurotic depressive reaction	Wt. loss Wt. gain	12 12	17 3	4.49	< 0.05
Endogenous depression	Wt. loss Wt. gain	6 3	1 1	Fisher test	N.S.
Neurotic depressive reaction	Wt. loss Wt. gain	8 9	16 2	5.34	< 0.05
No endogenous depression or neurotic depressive reaction	Wt. loss Wt. gain	31 24	8 7	0.04	N.S.
Anxiety state and/or anxiety phobic state	Wt. loss Wt. gain	11 11	9 4	1.23	N.S.
Depression included in overall diagnosis	Wt. loss Wt. gain	18 13	13 4	1.63	N.S.
Sad in last few weeks (Patient Questionnaire)	Wt. loss Wt. gain	28 27	21 4	6.60	< 0.02
Sadness (Psychiatrist rist questionnaire)	Wt. loss Wt. gain	13 10	15 4	2.35	N.S. (< 0.20)

** = two-tail test

depression', 'anxiety states', 'depression included in the overall diagnosis', or 'psychiatrist's rating of sadness'. The relationship between broken sleep and weight change in the last few weeks in the states 'quite a bit' and 'very' sad (Patient Questionnaire) separately was next examined (Table 61). This was done in order to check whether the relationship between weight change and sleep is contributed to by the difference between patients rating themselves 'quite a bit' and those rating themselves 'very' sad. It showed that in this instance the relationship between weight change and broken sleep is the same in the two categories.

In further analyses, the relationship between sleep in the last few weeks and weight change since the start of the illness (as opposed to weight change in the last few weeks) was explored. Similar results to those already described were obtained although the strength of the association was sometimes less. Thus, Table 62 shows a significant relationship between weight loss since the start of the illness and duration of sleep of $6\frac{1}{2}$ hours or less, and between weight gain

Table 61. 2 × 2 Contingency Table. The relationship between broken sleep in the last few weeks and weight change in the last few weeks in the states 'quite a bit' and 'very' sad (Patient Questionnaire)

Sad	Wt. change in last few weeks	Broken sleep (min.) 0	> 30	X²	p**
Quite a bit	Wt. loss Wt. gain	12 16	6 2	4.01	< 0.05
Very	Wt. loss Wt. gain	16 11	15 2	5.71	< 0.02

** = two-tail test

Table 62. 2 × 2 Contingency Table. The relationship between length of time asleep in the last few weeks (Interviewer Questionnaire) and weight change since the start of the illness (Interviewer Questionnaire) in different psychiatric states

Diagnosis and state of sadness	Wt. change since start of illness	Length of time asleep (hr) < 6½	> 7½	X²	p*
Endogenous depression and/or neurotic depressive reaction	Wt. loss Wt. gain	49 13	20 17	5.72	< 0.01
Endogenous depression	Wt. loss Wt. gain	11 3	9 8	1.94	N.S. (< 0.10)
Neurotic depressive reaction	Wt. loss Wt. gain	41 11	13 9	2.14	N.S. (< 0.10)
No endogenous depression or neurotic depressive reaction	Wt. loss Wt. gain	42 31	32 38	1.81	N.S. (< 0.10)
Anxiety state and/or anxiety phobic state	Wt. loss Wt. gain	32 11	21 16	2.04	N.S. (< 0.10)
Depression included in overall diagnosis	Wt. loss Wt. gain	52 15	20 19	6.68	< 0.005
Sad in last few weeks (Patient Questionnaire)	Wt. loss Wt. gain	67 28	31 28	4.34	< 0.02
Sadness (Psychiatrist Questionnaire)	Wt. loss Wt. gain	43 16	15 16	4.31	< 0.02

* = one-tail test

and sleep of $7\frac{1}{2}$ hours or more in the category 'endogenous depression and/or neurotic depressive reaction' ($p < 0.01$), 'depression included in the overall diagnosis' ($p < 0.005$), 'patients' rating of sadness' ($p < 0.02$) and 'psychiatrist's rating of sadness' ($p < 0.02$). A trend at the 10 per cent level in support of such a relationship is evident in 'endogenous depression', 'neurotic depressive reaction', 'no depression' and 'anxiety states'. The relationship between time of waking and weight change since the start of the illness appeared as close as that between time of waking and weight change in the last few weeks. However, the relationship between broken sleep and weight change in the last few weeks previously demonstrated in some of the psychiatric states disappears when change since the start of the illness is substituted for recent weight change.

The relationship between change in body shape since the start of the illness, (as opposed to absolute weight change), and sleep in each of the diagnoses and the state of sadness was then examined, using Quetelet's Index of body shape (Q.I.). The intercorrelational matrix had shown that this index had a correlation of 0.82 with weight, and in this study these two measures could probably have been interchanged with little effect on the results. Patients in whom Q.I. had increased or decreased by 0.20 or more were included. This is equivalent to a weight change of just over 10 pounds in a person of height 5 ft. 10 ins. The distribution table indicated that 79 patients exhibited such a decrease and 59 such an increase, this population being less than half the number showing weight change since the start of the illness. Table 63 shows that the relationship between decrease in Q.I. since the start of the illness and length of time asleep of $6\frac{1}{2}$ hours or less, and between increase of Q.I. since the start of the illness and length of sleep of $7\frac{1}{2}$ hours or more is significant in all diagnoses except 'no depression', 'anxiety states' and 'patients' rating of sadness'. This relationship was less clear when Q.I. was investigated in relation to time of waking in the last few weeks, where the only significant relationship to emerge occurred in the category 'no depression'. However a more striking relationship emerged, which had not been present in the case of weight change, between change in Q.I. since the start of the illness and the time of falling asleep in the last few weeks in the categories 'endogenous depression and/or neurotic depressive reaction' ($p < 0.02$), 'neurotic depressive reaction' ($p < 0.01$), 'depression included in the overall diagnosis' ($p < 0.05$) and 'psychiatrist's rating of sadness' ($p < 0.05$) (Table 64).

Finally, short and long sleepers were compared in respect of their maximum ever index of body shape. When 51 patients who reported sleeping for 5 hours or less in the last few weeks were compared with 61 patients sleeping $8\frac{1}{2}$ hours or more, there was no significant difference in the Q.I. maximum of the two groups. That is, maximum weight ever did not seem to bear a clear relationship to current duration of sleep.

Aspects of the relationship between sleep and skinfold thickness were then investigated in each of the psychiatric diagnoses and the state of sadness. Patients in whom measured triceps skinfold thickness was 10.0 mm or less and those in whom it was 25.0 mm or more were included, accounting for 71 and

Table 63. 2 × 2 Contingency Table. The relationship between length of time asleep in the last few weeks (Interviewer Questionnaire) and change in Quetelet's Index (Q.I.) since the start of the illness in different psychiatric states

Diagnosis and state of sadness	Change in Q.I. since start of illness	Length of time asleep (hr.) < 6½	> 7½	X²	p*
Endogenous depression and/or neurotic depressive reaction	Decrease QI > 0.20	23	5	15.13	< 0.0001
	Increase QI > 0.20	2	12		
Endogenous depression	Decrease QI > 0.20	4	0	Fisher test	< 0.05
	Increase QI > 0.20	2	5		
Neurotic depressive reaction	Decrease QI > 0.20	20	5	9.27	< 0.002
	Increase QI > 0.20	1	7		
No endogenous depression or neurotic depressive reaction	Decrease QI > 0.20	23	15	0.39	N.S.
	Increase QI > 0.20	17	15		
Anxiety state and/or anxiety phobic state	Decrease QI > 0.20	18	9	1.82	N.S. (< 0.10)
	Increase QI > 0.20	7	10		
Depression included in overall diagnosis	Decrease QI > 0.20	22	6	8.74	< 0.002
	Increase QI > 0.20	5	12		
Sad in last few weeks (Patient Questionnaire)	Decrease QI > 0.20	29	12	1.99	N.S. (< 0.10)
	Increase QI > 0.20	12	12		
Sadness (Psychiatrist Questionnaire)	Decrease QI > 0.20	24	4	9.99	< 0.002
	Increase QI > 0.20	5	10		

* = one-tail test

146

Table 64. 2 × 2 Contingency Table. The relationship between time of falling asleep in the last few weeks (Interviewer Questionnaire) and change in Quetelet's Index (Q.I.) since the start of the illness in different psychiatric states

Diagnosis and state of sadness	Change in Q.I. since start of illness		Time of falling asleep		X^2	p^{**}
			< 11.30 p.m.	> 1.00 a.m.		
Endogenous depression and/or neurotic depressive reaction	Decrease	QI > 0.20	7	14	6.62	< 0.02
	Increase	QI > 0.20	13	3		
Endogenous depression	Decrease	QI > 0.20	2	1	Fisher test	N.S.
	Increase	QI > 0.20	5	2		
Neurotic depressive reaction	Decrease	QI > 0.20	5	14	7.26	< 0.01
	Increase	QI > 0.20	8	1		
No endogenous depression or neurotic depressive reaction	Decrease	QI > 0.20	16	18	0.81	N.S.
	Increase	QI > 0.20	10	18		
Anxiety state and/or anxiety phobic state	Decrease	QI > 0.20	9	11	2.35	N.S. (< 0.20)
	Increase	QI > 0.20	9	3		
Depression included in overall diagnosis	Decrease	QI > 0.20	9	15	5.21	< 0.05
	Increase	QI > 0.20	14	4		
Sad in last few weeks (Patient Questionnaire)	Decrease	QI > 0.20	14	22	0.16	N.S.
	Increase	QI > 0.20	11	14		
Sadness (Psychiatrist Questionnaire)	Decrease	QI > 0.20	7	14	4.79	< 0.05
	Increase	QI > 0.20	12	4		

** = two-tail test

72 patients respectively. In the case of subscapular skinfold thickness, patients in whom the measurement was 10.0 mm or less, and those in whom it was 20.0 mm or more were included, and this accounted for 91 and 88 patients respectively. Although occasionally significant associations were found between skinfold thickness and broken sleep and time of awakening, in most instances there was no relation between skinfold thickness, a measure of adiposity, and sleep in either the psychiatric diagnoses or the state of sadness.

Reference

Crisp, A. H. and Stonehill, E. (1973). Aspects of the relationship between sleep and nutrition: a study of 375 psychiatric out-patients. *Br. J. Psychiat.*, **122**, 379–394.

CHAPTER 14

Discussion

The impairment of sleep in subjects with anorexia nervosa is strikingly located within the second half of the night and it has been suggested (Crisp, 1967) that this may reflect a reversion to more primitive sleep/activity patterns in the face of starvation, particularly of carbohydrate; also that such factors might contribute to disturbance of sleep associated with a variety of other conditions.

It is noteworthy that the EEG study within Study 1 revealed an increase of slow wave sleep which accounted for most of the total increase of sleep following substantial restoration of weight in subjects with anorexia nervosa. However, the ultimate levels of weight were somewhat below matched population mean levels, whilst at the same time carbohydrate had not figured prominently in the treatment diet. In a subsequent study (Lacey and coworkers, 1975) of a group of ten anorexia nervosa subjects before and after restoration of weight to strictly matched population mean levels in association with substantial carbohydrate intake, not only was the total amount of sleep increased but this was predominantly accounted for in terms of REM sleep.

Nevertheless not all anorectics achieve and maintain a low weight by abstaining solely from carbohydrate. Some achieve this by indiscriminate vomiting of ingested food which may instead contain normal or excessive amounts of carbohydrate as well as other food stuffs. These subjects, who thereby become more generally depleted—e.g. of proteins—are often amongst the most restless (as well as the most physically ill) of all anorectics. Such restlessness will also particularly pervade their sleep although they may deny this even more than most patients.

Recently Chen and coworkers (1974) have demonstrated a direct association between free tryptophan levels in the blood and the amount of REM sleep. The former are known to be influenced by immediate dietetic factors especially of a carbohydrate kind (Fernstrom and Wurtman, 1974). Furthermore one is reminded of the findings of Southwell, Evans and Hunt (1972) and Brezinova and Oswald (1972) showing that a bedtime hot milk cereal drink is associated with longer and less restless sleep in humans, and Fara, Rubinstein and Sonnenschein (1969), who found that fat introduced into the duodenum of cats enhanced their sleep. These latter authors postulated a probable role for a gastro-intestinal hormone in promoting sleep.

It is therefore probable that sleep is governed by a variety of dietetic factors which, within anorexia nervosa, are likely to be dramatically expressed in relation to the extreme forms of starvation that can arise. In obesity too, major weight and sleep changes may both be contributed to by the same dietetic factors.

In the second study a variety of measures were developed and standardized, as far as possible, so that enquiry could be aimed at various aspects of the problem. Attempts were made to control for interviewer bias and other factors, which it was felt might influence the variables to be measured. For example, height was measured so that weight and weight changes could be considered in terms of body shape. Patients were asked whether their reports of weight included clothing or not, so that this factor could be taken into account. Reports of the ingestion of psychotropic drugs and the presence of physical illness which might influence sleep were recorded and examined. The need to be wakened was recorded so that time of waking could be examined separately in a group reporting spontaneous waking. Great efforts were made to push the patient towards greater accuracy of report and in our view the methodology in this part of the study was particularly rigorous. However, in a study of this nature in which very many factors are involved, it has not proved possible to do justice to all of them.

An attempt has been made to select representative areas of reported behaviour, feelings and clinical judgement. In making this selection, use was made of the distribution patterns obtained and displayed in Chapter 11.

Thus the average reported duration of sleep *before the illness* was 7 hr. 16 min. This does not differ much from the average duration of sleep in the general population, which has usually been reported as about $7\frac{1}{2}$ hr. (Kleitman and coworkers, 1973; Tune, 1969). However, McGhie and Russell (1962) (see Chapter 1) have drawn attention to the wide variation in both the duration of sleep and its distribution in the normal population, and this is also true of the present psychiatric population. In this latter group, the average duration of sleep *in the last few weeks* had fallen by 24 min. to 6 hr. 52 min. This is also consistent with the findings of others (Weiss, Kasinoff and Bailey, 1962; Willis, 1965; McGhie, 1966; Ward, 1968) who have all reported (see Chapter 4) that sleep disturbance is a common feature in psychiatric illness and is not confined to affective disorders.

The average *time of falling asleep* in our population was significantly later in the *last few weeks* than *before the illness*, although the mean *time of going to bed*, which is one factor influencing time of falling asleep, was not different between the two periods. The average *duration of interrupted sleep* was significantly greater in the *last few weeks* than *before the illness*, but there was no difference in the mean *time of waking* although the distribution was different. One factor influencing *time of waking* is the need to be wakened because of having to get up. This may be important as more patients reported the need to be wakened before the illness than in the last few weeks, when some of them had probably stopped working, and this is consistent with the earlier average time reported for getting up before the illness. Thus, the greater average *time spent in bed* in the last few weeks is mainly contributed to by the later *time of getting up*. The average *overall sleep reduction* associated with psychiatric illness in this study consists, therefore, of *difficulty in falling asleep* and an *increase in interrupted sleep*, changes which have often been regarded as being associated with the diagnosis of anxiety state and neurotic depressive reaction (Mayer-Gross, Slater and Roth, 1969). The present findings are in contrast to the study by Kupfer, Detre and Harrow (1967) who found early morning waking, as opposed to initial insomnia and interrupted sleep, to be associated with an increase in symptoms in psychiatric patients.

More specifically we have found that, although patients with endogenous depression share with those with neurotic depression a tendency to waken earlier than those with anxiety states, they also go to bed earlier and fall asleep earlier than patients in all other categories. Indeed, the total amount of sleep is least amongst those with neurotic depression. In fact the overall sleep period of patients with endogenous depression occurs earlier within the 24-hour cycle than is the case with all other subjects and this is especially in contrast to subjects with anxiety state whose sleep period is shifted in the opposite direction. It would seem that this phenomenon may underlie the widespread, but from our study apparently false, assumption that subjects with severe forms of depression generally waken particularly early but do so within the context of very little overall sleep. It would appear rather that, with their sleep period shifting to an earlier position in the day, they inevitably waken earlier than other people, something of which they are likely to complain bitterly, since they waken in isolation and to such painful experiences each morning. Within our study there were also interesting tendencies for people categorized by tension to go to bed later than others but then to get off to sleep reasonably quickly, in contrast to those who displayed merely anxiety. Anger was the mood associated with least sleep and most broken sleep, whilst sadness was associated with going to bed early and early waking as would be expected to be the case in view of the similar findings in endogenous depression.

Although the average weight of patients was not different in the two periods under investigation, *a wide range of distribution of weight and weight change in both directions* was found. About a third of the population reported major weight change of 10 lbs or more since the start of the illness, and nearly half the patients reported some weight change in the last few weeks. Fluctuations in body weight are regarded as common in psychiatric illness, weight loss more commonly being described in association with illness, and weight gain with recovery (Jaspers, 1962). In the present study, weight loss was only slightly more frequent than weight gain, and it is possible that some patients were recovering at the time of attendance.

Although many patients were able to supply fairly clear reports of their sleep and weight and any changes thereof, it often proved more difficult to determine the time of onset of the illness. This appeared particularly so in patients whose symptoms manifested themselves as exaggerations of preexisting character traits. This is reflected in the Patient Questionnaire self-reports of feelings in which over a third of patients rated themselves as 'quite a bit' or 'very' *nervous, on top of the world, excited, sad, tense, fidgety and restless,* and *irritable,* in the time just before the present illness. However, ratings increased so that over two thirds of patients rated themselves 'quite a bit' or 'very' *nervous, sad, tense, fidgety and restless,* and *irritable* in the last few weeks. This is in contrast to the psychiatrists' ratings of feelings in which the category 'very' was seldom selected. As previously suggested, the tendency for higher self-ratings of mood by patients may reflect their subjective sense of extreme turmoil, consonant with their recent decision to seek help, as opposed to the clinician's frame of reference in which the patient is rated in comparison with others. In this connection it is noteworthy that ratings of 'very' were also rare in part 1 of the Psychiatrists' Questionnaire, the diagnostic profile. This is also likely to be accounted for partly by long waiting lists, usually about six weeks for new referrals, thus probably excluding some acutely disturbed patients.

Although our main aim was to explore the relationships, if any, between sleep and weight changes in the overall population, we have explored in depth not only those other associations referred to above but also the possibility of associations between nutritional characteristics and diagnosis of mood. Thus, in our population we have found no evidence for an association between a tendency to endogenous depression and a pyknic habitus in so far as this latter can be identified in terms of overall excessive fatness. Instead, such excessive fatness in the history was found to be strikingly associated with a tendency to major weight change, either weight loss *or* weight gain, within the illness, whatever the nature of the latter. In contrast, the characteristic of having once been thin was associated with a current diagnosis of neurotic depression, and also a self-report of very disturbed mood or being observed to be tense. A present state of thinness was also associated with the diagnosis of personality disorder and with being observed to be angry and/or tense. Thus little support is found for the notion of manic depressive illness being related to body build and we are in agreement over this with other researchers including Nicoletti, Magherini and Germano (1961) and Zersen, Koellet and Rey (1969). At the same time there is some suggestion that thinness is associated with neurotic disorder and character disorder.

Inspection of the intercorrelational matrix in conjunction with the distribution tables proved valuable by revealing the form of the data and thus providing guidance in the selection of items for further analyses aimed at exploring the main hypothesis. Owing to the many factors involved and their complex nature, large amounts of data were collected, although it was recognized that not all of them could be examined in detail in the final analyses. At this stage intercorrelations between patients' and interviewers' reports of sleep items, and between patients' and interviewers' reports of weight items, were revealed as high in all cases, ranging between $r = 0.84$ and $r = 0.90$. This allowed single measures of these items to be examined in relation to other items in the further analyses. The only item in which reports could be compared with direct measurement was present weight. The high correlations between patients' report and measured weight, and between interviewers' report and measured weight, r = 0.96 and 0.98 respectively, revealed the validity of such reports in this area. Significant, yet much lower, intercorrelations were obtained in some instances between items which are not so obviously related.

It was clear from the initial work on the development of the questionnaires that some questions produced more reliable and valid responses than others, and some responses were most unreliable and invalid and depended on how the questions were phrased. Even in the area of present weight, in which the correlation between measured weight and report was high, when a distribution table was prepared of reported weight as a percentage of measured weight, the reports of ten patients were revealed to be more than 10 per cent outside the measured weight. However, in spite of the doubt cast on the validity of reported information, the usefulness and importance of such information should be stressed, as it forms the basis of clinical psychiatric practice.

Inspection of data could not, of course, reveal whether the relationship between items which are significantly yet not obviously related is a direct one, or whether the relationship is indirect, both items being more closely related to a third item being measured. For example, in a study of 143 depressed patients Kiloh and Garside (1963) have found a significant intercorrelation of 0.20 between early morning waking and a weight loss of 7 lbs or more. However, both these items were found to be significantly associated with a diagnosis of endogenous depression. Similarly, Carney, Roth and Garside (1965) found a significant correlation of 0.23 between early morning waking and weight loss in 129 in-patients with depressive illness. Both items were found to be features of depression which responded to ECT. In both these studies the patients had been diagnosed as suffering from either endogenous depression or neurotic depressive reaction. The methodology of Kiloh and Garside's study has been criticized by McConaghy, Joffe and Murphy (1967), who suggested that these established diagnoses might influence clinicians, causing them to elicit symptoms believed to correspond to the diagnoses. The present study also revealed a significant, yet lower positive correlation, r = 0.18, between *waking earlier in the last few weeks* than before the illness and *weight loss in the last few weeks*. However, in contrast to the studies referred to above, attempts have been made in the design of the present study to control for bias by independently obtaining information in the three main areas under investigation. Nevertheless, clearly in our investigation as well, both *weight loss* and *time of waking* could be more closely associated with another item such as *sadness* or *depression*.

In order to further examine such interrelationships a principal components analysis was carried out on the intercorrelations between 30 items taken from the matrix. Items were selected after studying the intercorrelational matrix and were chosen to include a cross-section of information about nutrition, sleep and psychiatric state. An attempt was made to include some items which were significantly correlated but not obviously related as information. In an analysis of this kind in which information in different fields of the investigation was combined, it was not expected that a major factor would emerge, and this proved to be the case. As outlined in Chapter 13 the first 10 principal components were extracted. Component 1 revealed a weak association between patients' ratings of *unpleasant feelings* during the last few weeks and taking *longer to fall asleep* and the *need to be wakened*. Initial insomnia is traditionally associated with the diagnosis of anxiety state and neurotic depressive reaction (Mayer-Gross, Slater and Roth 1969), but these diagnoses were not present in this component. Furthermore, in this component difficulty in falling asleep was not associated with diminished sleep but rather with a shift in the time of the sleep period. Moreover we found that the average weight of the total population did not change significantly from before the illness to the last few weeks. These findings suggest the possibility that there may be an association between the subjective appreciation of unpleasant feelings such as *tension, anxiety, anger, irritability, sadness* and *restlessness* and *difficulty in falling asleep*, independent of specific psychiatric diagnosis and of nutritional factors.

It was expected that separate factors in the three fields of sleep, nutrition and psychiatric state would emerge (component 2 is a factor which consisted only of a number of aspects of sleep, component 4 consisted only of items of nutritional state, and components 6 and 7 of feeling states and psychiatric diagnosis), and the main interest within Study 2 is focused on the way in which items from the three areas combine.

Nevertheless the intercorrelations between various aspects of sleep highlight the complex determination of any one item which may often be ignored in the clinical situation. For example, *waking early* is significantly correlated with *falling asleep early*. Thus, early morning waking, which in clinical practice is usually arbitrarily defined as waking before a specific time, may sometimes reflect a shift in time of the sleep period without a diminution in the duration of the sleep. In other cases it is clear that early morning waking is associated with diminished sleep. Nevertheless time of waking, assessed independently of other aspects of sleep, is often regarded as useful in clinical practice. For example, reports of time of waking have been shown to be empirically useful in predicting ECT response in depressive illness (Carney, Roth and Garside, 1965). *Time of waking* has also been used in this study, no attempt being made to control for *time of going to bed or to sleep*, although in some analyses the *spontaneity or otherwise of waking* has been taken into account.

In contrast, components 3, 5 and 8 of the principal components analysis revealed an association between sleep items and nutritional items, although the loadings of some of the variates on these components were not high. In components 3 and 8, the association was between *weight loss* especially in the last few weeks and *diminished sleep*, although in both cases there was an increase in the *length of time spent in bed*. The sleep disturbance in component 3 was *interrupted sleep*, and in component 8 *initial insomnia*, together with *spontaneous waking*, the picture being complicated by the consumption of sleeping pills. Component 5, which revealed the converse association between *weight gain* and *increased sleep*, also included a shift in the sleep period towards *sleeping later*. The association between weight change and duration of sleep in these three components did not include significant loadings on ratings of mood, such as sadness, and psychiatric diagnoses, such as endogenous depression and neurotic depressive reaction.

Altogether these components revealed evidence of a link between nutrition and sleep, independent of mood or diagnosis, although components 1, 9 and 10 provided evidence in support of the traditionally held view of an association between sleep, mood and psychiatric state, independent of nutrition. The relationship between initial insomnia and patients' ratings of unpleasant feelings, revealed in component 1, has already been discussed. Component 9 displayed the converse of this situation. In this case, *falling asleep more quickly* was associated with subjective ratings of *feeling on top of the world* and *excited*, but the situation was complicated by the consumption of sleeping pills. It was not until the 10th component, which accounted for only 3.7 per cent of the variance, that a high loading for the diagnosis of *endogenous depression* emerged. This is in association with the psychiatrists' ratings of *sadness*, and ratings of *falling asleep quickly* and *spontaneous waking*. It is of note that patients' ratings of sadness, reports of weight loss and reports of waking earlier were not associated with this component.

The possibility had previously been considered that some psychiatrists might be influenced in making a diagnosis of endogenous depression by the presence of weight loss and early morning waking, independent of disturbed mood or other features of depression. Such a contingency would operate against the hypothesis being tested in this study. Component 10 lent no support to the belief that the psychiatrists were influenced in this way, although the absence of patients' ratings of sadness in this component is noteworthy. The likelihood of the psychiatrists being influenced in this way was probably partly dependent on whether or not they supported the view that there is a dichotomy of depressive cases into endogenous and neurotic varieties. Even if they viewed depressive illness along a single continuum, a distinction between endogenous depression and neurotic depression was imposed in the present study by the diagnostic profile. Each psychiatrist, therefore, was asked to provide his criteria, if any, for this distinction, with particular reference to vegetative phenomena. Two of the psychiatrists reported that they did support the dichotomous view of depression and regarded early morning waking as an important feature of endogenous depression, in contrast to the initial insomnia of neurotic depressive reaction. They regarded weight loss as a less important feature of endogenous depression. The other two psychiatrists reported that they supported the continuum view of depression but if asked to distinguish between endogenous depression and neurotic depression, as in this study, they both reported that they regarded weight loss and early morning waking as endogenous features. Thus for the purposes of this study early morning waking was regarded as an important feature of endogenous depression by all four psychiatrists and weight loss as an important feature by two of the psychiatrists.

Bearing on this point, an initial principal components analysis had been undertaken, based on the intercorrelations between 29 items on the first 300 patients, in which patients' information had been selected instead of inter-viewers' information, and the first five principal components had been extracted. Component 3 consisted of *weight loss* and *diminished sleep* in the form of *initial insomnia, broken sleep* and *spontaneous waking* but, in contrast to components 3 and 8 of the main analysis, they were associated with the diagnosis *neurotic depressive reaction*. In the light of the criteria reported by the psy-chiatrists for distinguishing between endogenous depression and neurotic depressive reaction, the association of neurotic depressive reaction but not of endogenous depression in this component was surprising. The high loading of neurotic depressive reaction is difficult to explain. It is possible that the psychiatrists were only influenced by major weight loss and sleep disturbance in differentiating between endogenous depression and neurotic depressive reaction, whereas less severe weight loss and sleep disturbance could have contributed to the loadings of these items on this factor. The other factors extracted are in agreement with the main principal components analysis. Components 1 and 5 consisted of items of feeling states and diagnoses only, and component 2 of sleep items only. In component 4, *endogenous depression* was associated with *obesity* (weight and skinfold thickness) as well as *early waking*. As in component 10 of the main principal components analysis, sleep was not thereby diminished but the sleep period was shifted and sleep was earlier.

Although the physiology of sleep is not completely understood, it is clear that a multitude of factors is important in the promotion and disturbance of sleep. The findings of the principal components analysis provided evidence in support of the existence of a link between nutritional factors and sleep in psychiatric patients. It also separately provided evidence in support of an association between emotional factors and sleep.

Following on from this analysis, the formation and analysis of 2×2 contingency tables has enabled the relationship between nutritional factors and aspects of sleep to be examined in separate feeling states and psychiatric diagnoses. By this method a significant relationship was revealed between *weight change in the last few weeks* and *length of time asleep* in the state of *sadness* and *each of the diagnoses*, except endogenous depression. In the contin-gency tables, the small number of patients diagnosed as having endogenous depression militates against statistically significant findings in this diagnosis; nevertheless in some tables when patients with endogenous depression were combined with patients with neurotic depressive reaction, the findings in the combined category became more highly significant than for neurotic depressive reaction alone. It is also true that stronger associations between weight change and sleep change were obtained in those states in which depression was diag-nosed than in such states as *absence of depression, anxiety* and *sadness*. Although, therefore, depression appeared to play a part in the relationship between weight change in the last few weeks and length of time asleep, it is particularly noteworthy that the link between weight change and sleep operated in both directions. Thus the significant association was also contributed to by patients displaying weight gain in conjunction with sleep of $7\frac{1}{2}$ hr. or more.

This association between weight gain and increase in sleep in depressive illness has been described in the literature (Michaelis, 1964). Although it is possible that in the categories *no depression* and *depression included in the overall diagnosis* in which severity was not rated, the association may have occurred in relation to recovery, in all other cases this is unlikely as only diagnoses and feeling states rated 'quite a bit' or 'very' were included.

Within Study 2 it has not been possible to examine the association between weight change and sleep in relation to all diagnoses and feeling states, but we have examined the relationship between duration of sleep and weight change in the last few weeks in each of the feeling states. In each case the association previously demonstrated within the state of *sadness* was significantly present except in the states of *on top of the world* and *excited* in which numbers were small.

It was only possible in this study to attempt to assess a few of the other factors which are likely to have an impact on sleep. Two such factors are the *consumption of psychotropic drugs causing drowsiness* and the presence of *physical illness* in which sleep is likely to be disturbed. Drugs causing drowsiness were widely consumed by the population under investigation and as a consequence numbers in the contingency tables, from which those patients taking drugs had been excluded, were small. Moreover the effect of drugs causing drowsiness is one which might be expected to mask a link between nutrition and sleep. In fact a strong association was still often found to exist although the possibility of the link being blurred in some instances cannot be discounted. Thus the relationship between weight change and duration of sleep was confirmed in *depression* and *sadness*, but no such relationship was revealed in the *absence of depression*.

Another important factor significantly related to duration of sleep is age (see Chapter 1). Thus McGhie and Russell (1962), in their survey of 2,500 adults, reported that with increasing age there is a decrease in the duration of sleep including initial insomnia, interrupted sleep and early morning waking, particularly in subjects over 65. Tune (1969) also reported a diminution in the mean duration of sleep in normal subjects with advancing age until the sixties, associated with early waking. However, in contrast to McGhie and Russell's (1962) study, he showed a significant tendency to fall asleep earlier. In the present study, age was not found to be a factor distinguishing between patients sleeping $6\frac{1}{2}$ hr. or less and those sleeping $7\frac{1}{2}$ hr. or more, or between patients waking at 6.30 a.m. or earlier and those waking at 7.30 a.m. or later. Indeed only 19 patients out of the total population were aged over 60 years.

Most of the contingency tables compared change in weight with an aspect of sleep in the last few weeks, as opposed to a change in that aspect of sleep. The data were initially examined in this way to reduce their complexity in the light of the large number and wide range of analyses to be performed. Nevertheless, if the main hypothesis on which this study was based was to be supported, then it would have been expected that change in weight would have been most closely linked to change in sleep. Our further analyses support this notion. Whereas no relationship was revealed between *weight change in the last few weeks* and *duration of sleep* in patients without depression, without physical illness and who were not taking drugs causing drowsiness, the relationship became significant in the predicted direction when *weight change* was compared with *change in the length of sleep.*

There was also a significant association in the predicted direction between weight change in the last few weeks and time of waking in all states except endogenous depression, neurotic depressive reaction and anxiety states, in which there was still a 10 per cent trend in the predicted direction. Indeed, as previously indicated, numbers with endogenous depression were small, and when this category was combined with neurotic depressive reaction the combined category generated a significant association. Thus, early morning waking and weight loss were found to be features of states apart from depression, and this supports the findings of McGhie (1966) and Willis (1965), who found that early morning waking was as common amongst in-patients not suffering from depression as those diagnosed as suffering from depressive illness.

It was considered likely that some patients would report waking early because they were wakened. Accordingly, an attempt was also made to assess and record reports of the *spontaneity or otherwise of waking.* However, the effect of this could only be sampled in this study and the state of sadness was chosen for this purpose. We have therefore studied the relationship of *change in time of spontaneous waking* between the last few weeks and before the illness and *weight change* in the last few weeks in patients rating themselves *more sad* in the last few weeks and in patients rating themselves *unchanged in sadness.* The predicted association between weight change and time of waking was again found. However, the association was stronger in patients rating themselves *sadder* than in patients rating themselves *unchanged in sadness,* suggesting that the mood of sadness is a factor influencing the association between weight change and time of waking. Once again it is noteworthy that the association operates in both directions. The evidence provided does indicate that the hypothesized link between weight change and time of waking was masked by the fact that waking in some patients was not spontaneous. Once again, the possibility cannot be discounted that this factor may have blurred such an association in some instances.

Meanwhile we have also found there to be no association between weight change in the last few weeks and time of falling asleep in any of the diagnoses or the state of sadness. A significant association between *weight loss in the last few weeks* and *broken sleep,* and between *weight gain in the last few weeks* and the *absence of broken sleep* was demonstrated in the states of *neurotic depressive reaction* and patients' rating of *sadness* only.

Thus it is possible that in the presence of depression and sadness a link between weight change and broken sleep exists. However, it was evident from experience gained during the administration of the questionnaires that assessment of the duration of broken sleep was the most difficult of the sleep items to measure, and it probably has less validity than most other sleep items. Once more in this instance other factors likely to have an impact on this aspect of sleep, such as the consumption of sleeping pills and occasions on which interruptions of sleep were not spontaneous, were not taken into account. Within such limitations, the contingency tables reveal an association in the predicted direction between *weight change* and *duration of sleep*, mainly contributed to by time of waking, and in some cases by interrupted sleep, but not at all by time of falling asleep.

Meanwhile the electroencephalographic evidence is that in depressive illness the sleep pattern is disturbed throughout the night (Diaz-Guerreo, Gottlieb and Knott, 1946, Oswald and coworkers, 1963), although it may be more severe during one or other part of the night. Thus although the concepts of 'initial insomnia' and 'early morning waking' remain popular and are useful in clinical practice, the distinction made by Hinton (1962) between patients who obtain more sleep in the first part of the night and those who sleep more in the second half of the night, and vice versa, would seem more valid. We would also claim that the association between sleep and nutrition that we have demonstrated can be regarded as mainly between weight change and sleep in the second half of the night.

We also examined the relationship between *weight change since the start of the illness* and aspects of sleep in the last few weeks in different psychiatric diagnoses and the state of sadness. The findings were in general agreement with the findings previously discussed in connection with *weight change in the last few weeks*, with strong associations between weight change since the start of the illness and duration of sleep emerging in many of the diagnoses and the state of sadness. A weaker association between weight change since the start of the illness and sleep in the last few weeks than between weight change in the last few weeks and sleep in the last few weeks is to be expected. It is likely that changes in sleep would be fairly closely associated in time with changes in weight and vice versa. It is probable that in some patients weight change since the start of the illness occurred early in the illness, there being no change in weight in the last few weeks. It is even possible that in some cases weight change since the start of the illness was associated with a lesser amount of weight change in the opposite direction in the last few weeks. Although these latter data may include some patients in whom both weight loss and weight gain since the start of the illness occurred, patients who reported both weight loss and weight gain in the last few weeks were excluded from the earlier tables. It is therefore somewhat surprising that the association between *weight change since the start of the illness* and *time of waking in the last few weeks* was in most cases as close as the association between *weight change in the last few weeks* and *time of waking*. The larger number of patients included in the former analysis is one factor which may account for this. The absence of an association between *time of falling asleep* in the few weeks and *weight change since the start of the illness* was in agreement with the lack of association between *weight change in the last few weeks* and *time of falling asleep*. The association between *broken sleep* and *weight change in the last few weeks*, demonstrated in *neurotic depressive reaction* and patients' ratings of *sadness*, was no longer present when *weight change since the start of the illness* was examined in relation to *broken sleep*, and this is not surprising for the reasons discussed above.

We also investigated the relationship between change in *Quetelet's Index* (Q.I.) of 0.20 or more since the start of the illness and aspects of sleep in the different diagnoses and the state of sadness. Q.I. and weight were highly correlated ($r = 0.82$). For instance a change in Q.I. of 0.20 usually represented a weight change of 8–10 lb. depending on height. Thus, although there are slight differences amongst individuals between weight change and the corresponding amount of change in Q.I., these measures were used almost interchangeably in this study, the measure having little bias in relation to height. For the purposes of this study then, change in Q.I. of 0.20 or more was regarded as major weight change. Although numbers of patients in the Q.I. analysis were thereby generally less than half the numbers considered in respect of corresponding analysis of weight change since the start of the illness, it is nevertheless evident that major weight change occurred not only in association with depression but also in other clinical states. Thus *major weight change* had a striking association with *duration of sleep*, except in the absence of depression, in which there was no association, and in anxiety states and patients' ratings of sadness, in which there was only a trend at the 10 per cent level in the predicted direction. It is therefore surprising, in the light of the earlier results, that a lack of association between *major weight change since the start of the illness* and *time of waking in the last few weeks* in all states except the absence of depression, should have emerged. In contrast to the previous findings, an association between *major weight change since the start of the illness* and *time of falling asleep in the last few weeks*, in the states of *depression* and patients' ratings of *sadness*, was revealed. This apparent association between major weight change and time of falling asleep, in contrast to the overall association between other measures of weight change and time of waking, is difficult to explain. It may be that whereas weight change and time of waking are linked, amount of weight change is not an important factor in this link. This seems improbable in the light of findings from Study 1 wherein *amount* of weight gain was significantly correlated with later time of waking in anorexia nervosa patients undergoing treatment. The possibility of the link between major weight change and time of falling asleep being spurious cannot be discounted, for it may be that the majority of patients who underwent major weight change did so early in their illness at a time remote from the last few weeks, during which time sleep was assessed.

Finally there was a singular lack of association between skinfold thickness and sleep in the majority of analyses. In four instances an association was present which reached statistical significance. In three of these cases, the relationship was between greater adiposity and more sleep, and between lesser adiposity and less sleep, and in one case the converse relationship held. It is difficult to interpret these findings. In the light of the large number of calculations carried out, one would expect some results to be significant by chance. Overall these results suggest that, in this population, there is little relationship between subscapular and triceps skinfold thickness, a measure of adiposity in these parts of the body, and sleep.

We recognize that the variables measured in this study are influenced by many factors and that the tools used in this enquiry have severe limitations. A general interpretation of the findings is therefore made with caution. The overall results provide further evidence of the existence of a link between nutrition and sleep. The nutritional factor revealed was weight change, and this was mainly associated with a difference in sleep affecting the second half of the night. Thus weight gain was often associated with sleeping longer and waking later, and weight loss with sleeping less and waking early. The thesis that weight and sleep changes are both variables dependent on mood and linked primarily through disturbance in mood or psychiatric state, has not generally been borne out in this study. The link between weight and sleep was shown to often transcend specific psychiatric diagnosis and mood state. Moreover when an association between weight change and sleep was demonstrated in one clinical state but not another, the association usually operated in both directions. Furthermore, within Study 1 we have demonstrated an association between weight change and sleep which was found to be closer than the association of either disturbed mood or depression; evidence which supports the findings of the second study. However, unlike Study 1, Study 2 does not provide much evidence of a quantitative link between weight change and sleep although in conjunction with other studies it does suggest that changes in weight and sleep are closely associated in time. Neither does Study 2 provide any answer to the question of whether the nutritional disturbance promotes the sleep disturbance or vice versa. However, in the light of the evidence, provided by Study 1, of the link between nutrition and sleep in anorexia nervosa, in which the nutritional disturbance is believed to be primary, it is also likely in a general psychiatric population in which there is weight change and sleep disturbance, that nutritional disturbance usually promotes the sleep disturbance. This notion is also in agreement with the animal experimental literature, in which enforced starvation promotes increased activity and diminished sleep as detailed in Chapter 5. The mechanisms of this link between weight change and sleep duration remain obscure, although it seems likely that the pathway involves diencephalic centres.

It is noteworthy in this connection that Pollitt (1965) has proposed the existence of a 'functional shift' which he believes operates at a hypothalamic level to generate the syndrome of 'endogenous' depression in predisposed subjects. Major features of the shift include early morning waking and weight loss. As a consequence of our studies we wish to suggest that some patients with 'psychiatric' disorders enter a state of reduced food intake which leads to weight loss. Such changes, if they become substantial, will then be associated with disruption of sleep, particularly in the second half of the night. This restlessness may also become a feature of waking life, especially in the early part of the day when it may become linked with anxiety and be displayed as agitation. It was Hinton (1963) who found this association of impaired sleep in the second half of the night with agitation as a feature of some depressed subjects whatever their diagnostic subcategory. Reduction in libido may also be expected to be a feature of this 'starving' posture (Crisp, 1965, 1967) and also constipation. This is not to deny that other factors can also contribute to these aspects of psychiatric disorder, which will of course anyway be coloured by the patient's primary morbid preoccupations, indeed our own study indicates that moods such as anxiety and anger independent of nutritional disturbance are probably importantly associated with sleep disturbance and this is the experience of all of us. For instance, anxiety is associated with difficulty in getting off to sleep, whilst anger tends to be associated with a reduced amount of sleep. Nevertheless an important link between 'adequate' nutrition and 'normal' sleep exists, and its disturbance mav contribute to the phenomenology of many psychiatric illnesses, both in terms of weight and sleep changes themselves and also related changes such as increased wakeful activity and constipation. These in their turn are likely to provide a focus of confirmation of the subject's fears and thereby reinforce them, sometimes thereby translating doubt into certainty (Figure 52).

It remains to be determined why some subjects lose so much weight, others gain so much and others do not change their weight during such illness. Such

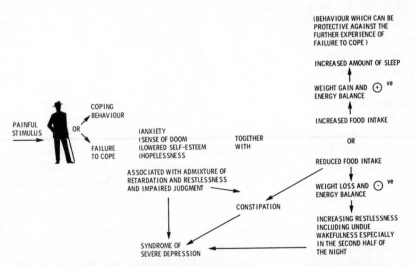

Figure 52. Diagrammatic representation of one way in which a nutritional factor might sometimes contribute to the evolution of the typical syndrome of severe depression associated with weight loss and early morning waking, and also the less common syndrome of depression, weight gain and hypersomnia

weight changes when they occur are likely to be mainly related to changes in food intake. It is, of course, the Kleinian branch of psychoanalytic theory which has directed most attention to possible relationships between the oral infantile experience (at which stage the infant is usually displaying a predominantly nutritionally based rest/activity cycle) and subsequent personality development and vulnerability to psychiatric illness. The present study, whilst not purporting to throw any light upon this school of thought, has served to show not only a basic immediate relationship between weight change and sleep but also a series of other relationships between shape, mood, diagnosis and sleep. Thus, whilst there appears to be little evidence for the notion that pyknic subjects (defined in terms of maximum ever fatness) are more prone to depressive illness than other kinds of psychiatric illness, it is noteworthy that the most pyknic subjects thus defined are also the most prone to display substantial lability of weight, either gain or loss, within their illness. Furthermore those, both male and female, with neurotic depressive illness will report having been thinner than others in times past. It is also perhaps noteworthy that an increasing number of researchers are showing that massively obese males but not females are significantly less depressed and in some instances less anxious than non-obese males (Simon, 1962; Silverstone, 1968; Crisp and McGuinness, 1975).

The strands within these various and separate approaches to an examination of the relationship between fatness and some psychiatric illness, especially perhaps depression, deserve greater conjoined attention and may yet be found to come together in a meaningful way.

Meanwhile, to revert to the more immediate relationship between sleep and nutrition emerging from the present study, it is striking how many authors have drawn attention to the link between nutritional disturbance and the hypersomniac and narcoleptic syndromes. Thus narcolepsy has been found to be frequently precipitated by meals and possibly to be more common in obese and weight labile subjects. McDonald Critchley (1962) emphasizes the presence of obesity in the syndrome of periodic hypersomnia and megaphagia which he described at that time. These subjects' attitudes to food and their irritable and detached manner are suggestive of the obese subject convalescent from anorexia nervosa and attempting, through dissociative mechanisms, to avoid further eating. Nonetheless some such subjects do eventually still eat themselves into a stupor, at which time they may then, through fluid retention in particular, display bizarre behaviour associated with EEG changes. In the present authors' view, the role therefore of nutritional factors in determining some of the features of this group of disorders, may sometimes be important and account for the rich diversity of symptomatology within them which has been outlined in Chapter 3. These syndromes in particular may reflect one end of the spectrum of presentation of disorders of sleep, weight and mood which in other settings would be more likely to be labelled as a psychiatric illness or a neurological disorder.

References

Brezinova, V. and Oswald, I. (1972). Sleep after a bedtime beverage. *Br. med. J.*, **2**, 431–433.
Carney, M. W. P., Roth, M. and Garside, R. F. (1965). The diagnosis of depressive syndromes and the prediction of ECT response. *Br. J. Psychiat.*, **111**, 659–674.
Chen, C. N., Kalucy, R. S., Hartmann, M. K., Lacey, J. H., Crisp, A. H., Bailey, J. E., Eccleston, E. G. and Coppen, A. (1974). Plasma, tryptophan and sleep. *Br. med. J.*, **4**, 564–566.
Crisp, A. H. (1965). Clinical and therapeutic aspects of anorexia nervosa—A study of 30 cases. *J. psychosom. Res.*, **9**, 67–78.
Crisp, A. H. (1967). The possible significance of some behavioural correlates of weight and carbohydrate intake. *J. psychosom. Res.*, **11**, 117–131.
Crisp, A. H. and McGuinness, B. (1975). Jolly fat. *Br. med. J.*, **4**, (In Press).
Critchley, M. (1962). Periodic hypersomnia and megaphagia in adolescent males. *Brain*, **85**, 627–656.
Diaz-Guerrero, R., Gottlieb, J. and Knott, J. (1946). The sleep of patients with manic-depressive psychoses, depressed type: An electroencephalographic study. *Psychosom. Med.*, **8**, 399–404.
Fara, J. W., Rubinstein, E. H. and Sonnenschein, R. R. (1969). Visceral and behavioural responses to intraduodenal fat. *Science*, **166**, 110–111.
Fernstrom, J. D. and Wurtman, R. J. (1974). Nutrition and the brain. *Sci. Am.*, **230**, 84–91.
Hinton, J. M. (1962). Sleep and motility in depressive illness. *Proc. R. Soc. Med.*, **55**, 907–910.
Hinton, J. M. (1963). Patterns of insomnia in depressive illness. *J. Neurol. neurosurg. Psychiat.*, **26**, 184–189.
Jaspers, K. (1962). *General Psychopathology* (Eds. Hoenig, J. and Hamilton, M. W.) Manchester University Press, Manchester.
Kiloh, L. G. and Garside, R. F. (1963). The independence of neurotic depression and endogenous depression. *Br. J. Psychiat.*, **109**, 451–463.
Kleitman, N., Mullin, F. J., Cooperman, N. R. and Titelbaum, S. (1973). *Sleep Characteristics*, University of Chicago Press, Chicago.
Kupfer, D. J., Detre, T. and Harrow, M. (1967). Relationship between sleep disorders and symptomatology. *Archs. gen. Psychiat.*, **17**, 710–716.
Lacey, J. H., Crisp, A. H., Kalucy, R., Hartmann, Margot and Chen, C. (1975) Weight gain and the sleeping EEG. *Br. med. J.*, **4**, (In Press).
Mayer-Gross, W., Slater, E. and Roth, M. (1969). *Clinical Psychiatry* (Eds. Slater, E. and Roth, M.) Balliere, Tindall and Cassel, London.
McConaghy, N., Joffe, A. D. and Murphy, B. (1967). The independence of neurotic and endogenous depressions. *Br. J. Psychiat.*, **113**, 479–484.
McGhie, A. M. (1966). The subjective assessment of sleep patterns in psychiatric illness. *Br. J. med. Psychol.*, **39**, 221–230.
McGhie, A. M. and Russell, S. M. (1962). Subjective sleep disturbance in the normal population. *J. ment. Sci.*, **108**, 642–644.
Michaelis, R. (1964). Depressive verstimmung und schlafsucht. *Arch. Psychiat. NervKrankh.*, **206**, 345–355.
Nicoletti, I., Magherini, G. and Germano, G. (1961). Richerche fattoriali sulla tipologia morfologica nella psicosi maniaco-depressiva comparativamente alle schizofrenia ebefreniche. *Riv. Neurobiol.*, **1**, 3.
Oswald, I., Berger, R. J., Jamarillo, R. A., Keddie, K. M. G., Olley, P. G. and Plunkett, G. B. (1963). Melancholia and barbiturates: a controlled EEG, body and eye movement study of sleep. *Br. J. Psychiat.*, **109**, 66–78.
Pollitt, J. (1965). *Depression and its Treatment*, William Heinemann Medical Books, London, pp. 34, 35.
Silverstone, J. T. (1968). Psychosocial aspects of obesity. *Proc. R. Soc. Med.*, **61**, 371–375.

Simon, R. I. (1963). Obesity as a depressive equivalent. *J. Am. med. Ass.*, **183**, 208.

Southwell, P. R., Evans, C. R. and Hunt, J. N. (1972) Effect of a hot milk drink on movements during sleep. *Br. med. J.*, **2**, 429–431.

Tune, G. S. (1969). Sleep and wakefulness in 509 normal human adults. *Br. J. med. Psychol.*, **42**, 75–80.

Ward, J. A. (1968). Alterations of sleep patterns in psychiatric disorder. *Can. psych. Ass. J.*, **13**, 249–257.

Weiss, H. R., Kasinoff, B. H. and Bailey, M. A. (1962). An exploration of reported sleep disturbance. *J. nerv. ment. Dis.*, **134**, 528–535.

Willis, J. H. P. (1965). Insomnia in psychiatric patients. *Guy's Hosp. Rep.*, **114**, 249–255.

Zersen, D., Koeller, D. M. and Rey, E. R. (1969). Objectivierende untersuchungen zur prämorbiden persönlichkeit endogen depressiver. In H. Hippins and H. Selback (Eds.), *Das Depressive syndrom*, Urban und Schwarzenberg, Munchen.

Conclusions

1. The present studies have served to confirm beyond all reasonable doubt that patients with anorexia nervosa experience reduced amounts of sleep especially within the second half of the night. Furthermore that this is a function of their impaired nutritional status. The same factor is probably operative amongst obese subjects losing weight on a low calorie diet whose sleep also becomes similarly changed.

2. Within a large population of out-patients suffering between them a variety of psychiatric disorders there appear to be very complicated but significant relationships between nutrition, sleep, mood and psychiatric diagnosis.
   Thus,

   (i) A history of obesity confers:
      (a) A propensity for *major weight change* (*increase or decrease*) during the illness *whatever its nature*.
      (b) No specific association with current *endogenous depression* or manic depressive psychosis.
   (ii) A history of having *once been thin* confers a tendency currently to have *neurotic depression* and/or *very disturbed mood* especially *tension*.
   (iii) A history of *weight loss* during *present illness* is more likely to have arisen in *neurotic depression/anxiety state* than in *endogenous depression*.
   (iv) A *present* state of *thinness* is more likely to be present amongst those with the diagnosis of *personality disorder* and who are *tense/angry* rather than in those who are *anxious/sad*.
   (v) A population of *psychiatrically ill people* overall display a tendency to report having not changed their time of going to bed or time of waking but take *longer to go to sleep*, have *more broken sleep* and *less total sleep* than before the illness.

   However, there are differences in subpopulations in this respect.
   (vi) Thus, more specifically:
      (a) Time of *going to bed* and *falling asleep* is *earlier* in *endogenous depression* than in the other diagnoses.
      (b) *Time of waking* is *early* in *endogenous depression* and *late* in *anxiety state* compared with the total psychiatric population.

(c) *Total sleep* is *less* amongst patients with *neurotic depression* than the other diagnoses, and *greatest* in those having *endogenous depression*.

(d) The sleep period in *endogenous depression* occurs earlier within the 24-hour cycle than is the case with the overall population and this contrasts with the later sleep periods of subjects with *neurotic depression* and *anxiety state*.

(vii) There are also tendencies for:

(a) *Going to bed later* to characterize those who are *tense*.

(b) For those who are *tense*, once in bed to fall asleep *more quickly*, and those who are *anxious* to take longer to fall asleep than others.

(c) For *broken sleep* to characterize those who are *angry*.

(d) For *going to bed early* and *early waking* to characterize those who are *sad*.

(e) For *least total sleep* to characterize those who are *angry*.

(viii) Within the total population of 375 subjects and irrespective of diagnosis, there is an important association, especially in relation to the previous few weeks, between *changes in weight* and *changes in sleep*. *Weight loss* is associated with a *reduction of total sleep*, compounded of more broken sleep and earlier waking. *Weight gain* is associated with an *increase in total sleep* compounded of *less broken sleep* and *later waking*.

3. It is finally concluded that:

(i) Changes in weight in psychiatric illness relate to an underlying history of and propensity for obesity. Furthermore, that these changes during the illness play a part in generating the sleep changes in the second half of the night which can come to be a feature of psychiatric illness. In contrast, the specific nature of the psychiatric illness does not appear to be associated either with a history of obesity (including pyknic habitus) or with a particular sleep pattern in the second half of the night although those who have neurotic depression and tension are more likely to have a history of a present state of thinness.

(ii) In contrast to this, sleep changes in the first half of the night are largely unrelated to weight changes and shape characteristics. They are strikingly related to disturbances of mood.

(iii) In other illnesses in which weight changes occur and/or which are characterized by such features as obesity or emaciation, we suggest that associated sleep disturbances may sometimes be dependent upon these nutritional factors. This underlying process may then sometimes operate in such syndromes as narcolepsy, Kleine-Levin syndrome, periodic hypersomnia and megaphagia as well as common obesity, anorexia nervosa and other wasting conditions.

Author Index

Subject Index

Activity,
  anorexia nervosa and, 22
  anxiety and, 40
  measurement of, 55, 57, 61
    Study I, 71
  nocturnal, psychiatric illness and, 34, 40
  obesity and, 19, 83
  prolonged starvation and, 47, 50
  psychiatric illness and, 40
  sexual, obesity and, 19
  waking, 13
Anorexia nervosa, 17, 21, 66, 68
  activity and, 22
  mood and, 22
  nocturnal motility and, 75
  relationship to hypersomnia and megaphagia, 26
  sleep and, 21, 149
  Study I, 73
  weight gain and, 73
Anxiety,
  restlessness and, 40
Appetite,
  animal studies, 44
  depression and, 33
  depression and hypersomnia, 41
  hypothalamus and, 44
  insomnia and, 31
  Kleine Levin syndrome and, 26
  megaphagia and hypersomnia, 25
  mood and, 20
  psychiatric illness and, 33

Body shape,
  measurement of, 59

Cyclical activity, 2

Daytime activity,
  psychiatric illness and, 40
Depression, 32
  'endogenous', 35, 41
  hypersomnia and, 41
  measurement of, 61

  'neurotic', 35
  obesity and, 33
  phenomenology of, 32
  restlessness and, 40
  weight gain, hypersomnia and, 26
  weight loss and, 33
Diet,
  measurement of, 60
  sleep and, 46, 47

Electroencephalogram,
  depression and, 158
  obesity and, 89
  sleep and, 11, 54
  sleep, anorexia nervosa and, 77
  sleep Study I, 148
Eysenck Personality Inventory, 61
  anorexia nervosa and, 74
  obesity and, 83
  use of, Study I, 72

Fatness,
  measurement of, 59
    Study II, 99
  psychiatric diagnosis and, 151, 162
    Study II, 118
Feeding,
  and depression, 2, 4
  and growth rate, 2
  in infancy, 1
  mood, mother and, 20
  mother and, 1
  sleep in animals and, 45
Food, sleep and, 148
  Study II, 138

Hypersomnia, 25
  depression and, 41
  nutrition and, 162
  psychiatric illness and, 34
Hypothalamus,
  appetite and, 44

Insomnia, 30
  hunger and, 31
  mood and, 30